Pirates

Shuky ★ Gorobei

Author: Shuky **Illustrator**: Gorobei **Translation**: Adam Marostica
This book is a translation of the original *Pirates 1* © Makaka Editions

ISBN : 978-0-9997698-8-1 Library of Congress Control Number: 2019903162

Published by Van Ryder Games and printed by Avenue 4 in China. Second Printing.

Find printable character records and other Graphic Novel Adventures at www.VanRyderGames.com

THERE HE IS.
IN THE WATER!

GET HIM BEFORE
THE SHARKS DO.
HURRY!!
AND TAKE HIM ALIVE.
HE'S THE ONLY ONE
WHO KNOWS WHERE
THE TREASURE IS.
GO! GO FASTER!

Strength: 13
Agility: 4
Intelligence: 5
Charisma: 8
Strength: 4
Agility: 10
Intelligence: 13
Charisma: 3
Strength: 5
Agility: 13
Intelligence: 8
Charisma: 4
HE CAN'T BE FAR. IT WOULD BE BETTER TO SPLIT UP... EACH OF US TAKE ONE DIRECTION!
Choose your character, read the rules, and fill in your character sheet before beginning at panel 1.

Rules

Dear pirate,

You have found yourself tasked with discovering the hiding place of the escaped prisoner. It really couldn't be easier...

During your adventure, take whichever path you wish to follow using the numbers indicated (and sometimes hidden) in each frame. Frame by frame, puzzle by puzzle, you'll find clues as to the whereabouts of the fugitive.

But watch out! These clues must be earned, and you will need to pay close attention if you hope to find them!

Observation is the magic word if you wish to avoid unfortunate surprises, as the island is teeming with danger: traps, ferocious creatures, enemies... And do not hesitate to take notes and form a plan during your journey, so that you don't find yourself going in circles... danger is everywhere! Keep your eyes peeled, there are hidden passages and useful objects for those keen enough to spot them. Speaking of which, you have the freedom to pick up what you like during your journey: you can carry a number of objects equal to your character's Strength value.

Whenever you like, you may drop any object you are carrying in order to pick up another. Feathers and gold pieces, however, don't take up any room in your inventory... just as well, as you're going to be needing a lot of them to succeed in your adventure.

Finally, keep in mind that the objects you have in your inventory at the end of this adventure could end up being useful on your next mission, Pirates: The City of Skulls. Even fruits, pebbles, and green leaves might come in handy!

Before your adventure you can find printable character sheets at www.VanRyderGames.com available as a full page or bookmark.

Now, it's time for your adventure!

Character Sheet

Character Name: ....

Strength [ ] **Agility** [ ] **Intelligence** [ ] **Charisma** [ ]

Collected Objects *(you may not carry more objects than your strength value)*

Light Objects *(objects with zero weight)*

Learned Techniques and Read Books

Notes

Resume at Frame [ ]

001

67
30

002

42

003

All that for this: an impasse! Make a U-turn to 54.

004

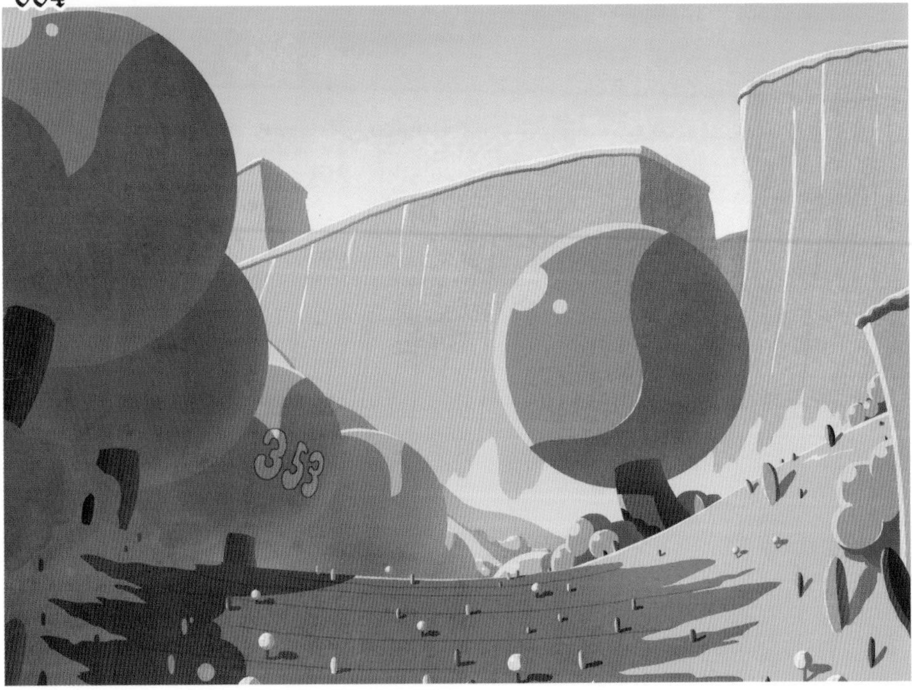
353

005

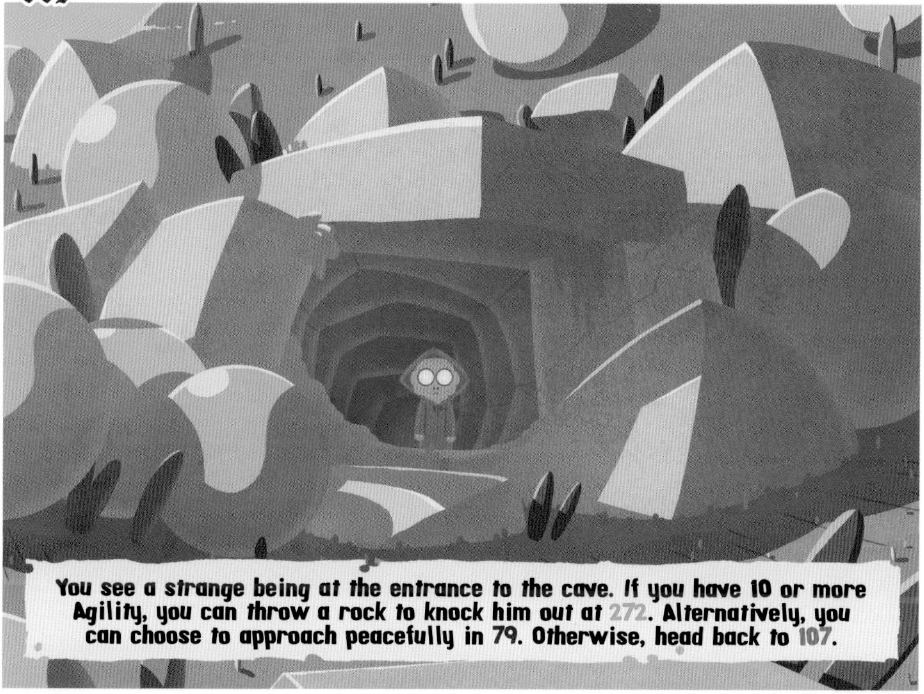
You see a *strange* being at *the* entrance to *the* cave. If you have 10 or more Agility, you can throw a rock to knock him out at 272. Alternatively, you can choose to approach peacefully in 79. Otherwise, head back to 107.

006

247
127
57

007

I'M FED UP! I'VE DONE EVERYTHING RIGHT, BUT NOTHING'S GROWING! MY BROTHERS KEEP MOCKING ME. YOU WOULDN'T HAPPEN TO HAVE ANY IDEAS, WOULD YOU?
Think: what could help this man to reap a healthy crop, like that of his brothers? Once you have an answer (only one!), go to 221.

008

222

009

You can turn back to 215, or if you have 10 or more Agility, speed through the forest to 33.

010

You can still turn back and return to 294. Otherwise, head to 24.

011

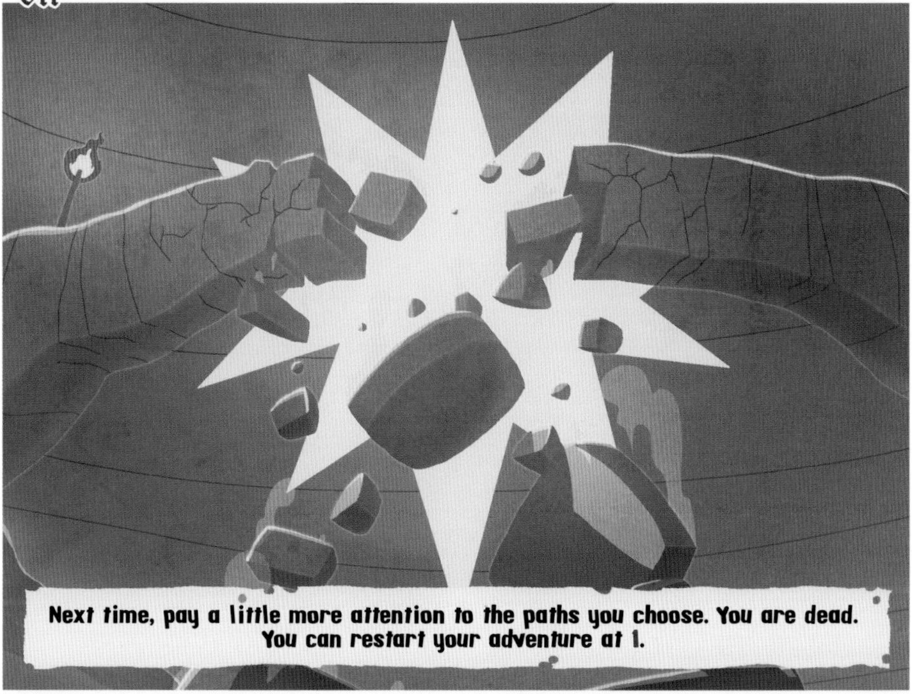
Next time, pay a little more attention to the paths you choose. You are dead.
You can restart your adventure at 1.

012

If you've collected at least twelve bananas, give them to the chief
and go to 308. Otherwise, go to 180.

013

183

014

183
155

015

95
↑ ↑
6 0

016

Return to 131.

017

THE ANSWER WAS "A LEAF", CLEARLY.
If you found the answer, go to 227. If not, go to 354.

018

Phew, good eye! You almost took a huge branch to the head!
131

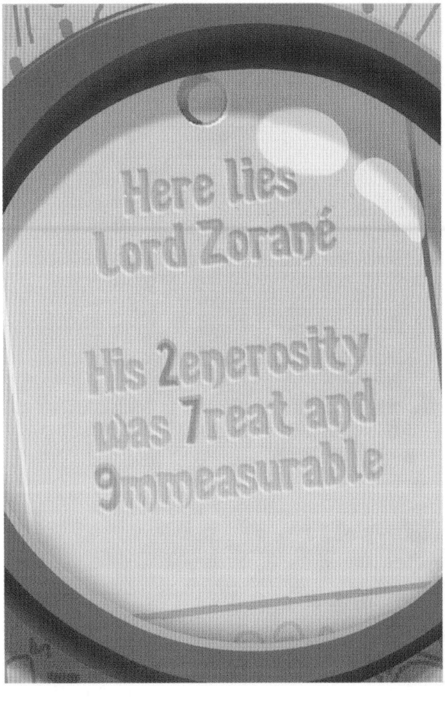
Here lies
Lord Zorané
His 2enerosity
was 7reat and
9mmeasurable

019

111

020

195

021

208
299

022

66
139

023

You have paid the ultimate price at the hands of a very stressed out indiginous resident of the island... you can begin anew at 1.
HOW MANY TIMES DO I HAVE TO TELL YOU NOT TO SHOOT PEOPLE IN THE BACK?
I...
SHUSH! I DON'T WANT TO HEAR IT! THAT'S SEVEN TIMES THIS WEEK. YOU'RE EXHAUSTING!

024

The vegetation is far too dense. You'll never make it through.
Retrace your steps to 294.

025

46
249

You are now holding the most coveted object on the island: the map! It will allow you to make your way around the island much safer than before. You can start using it immediately.

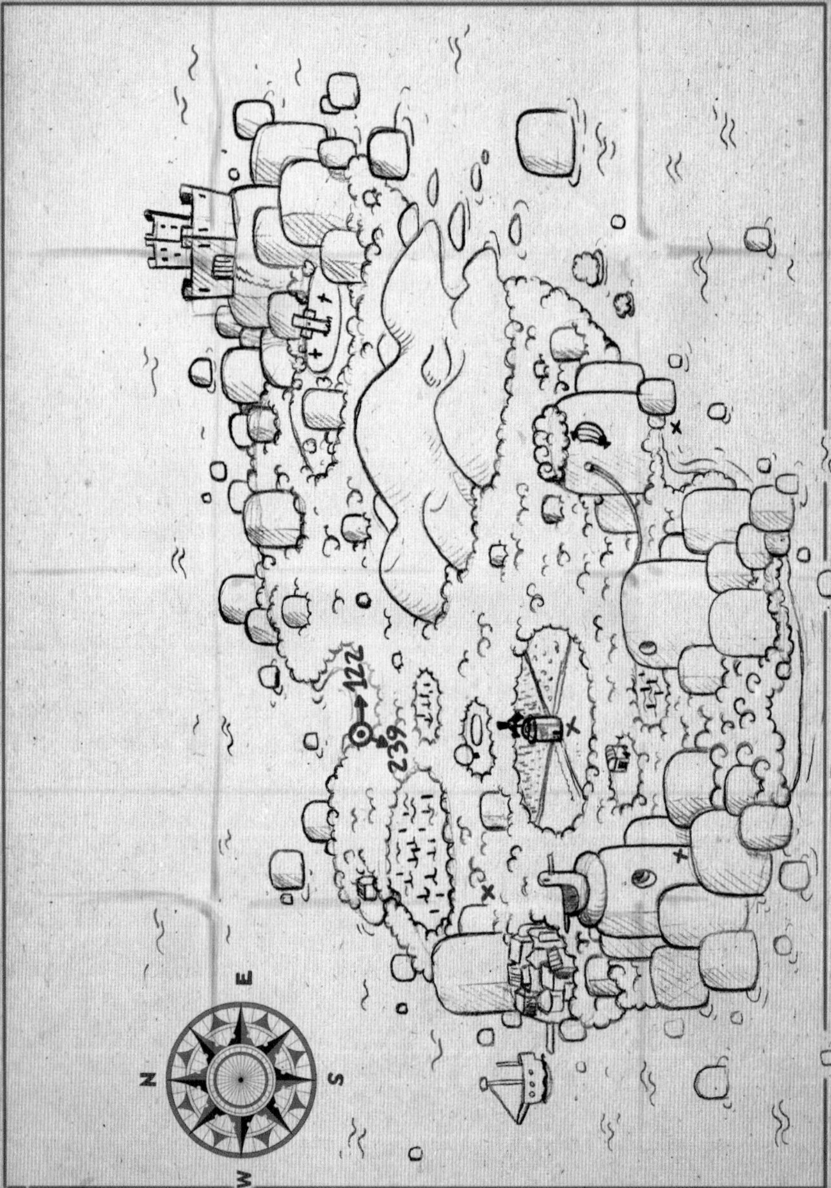
122
239
N
E
S
W

027

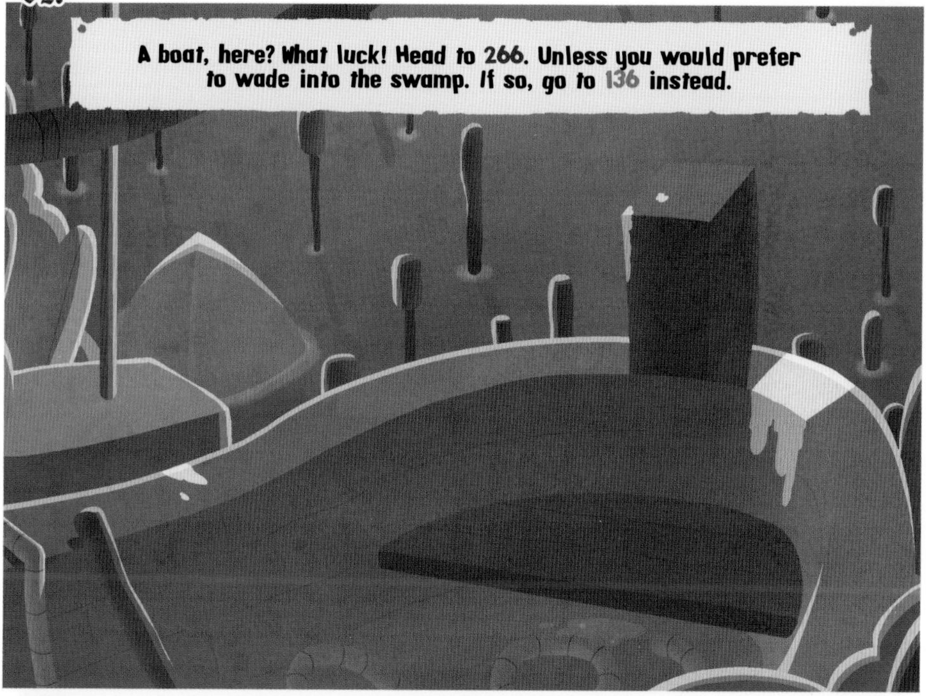
A boat, here? What luck! Head to 266. Unless you would prefer to wade into the swamp. If so, go to 136 instead.

028

165
203
343↑
36

029

210
95
223

030

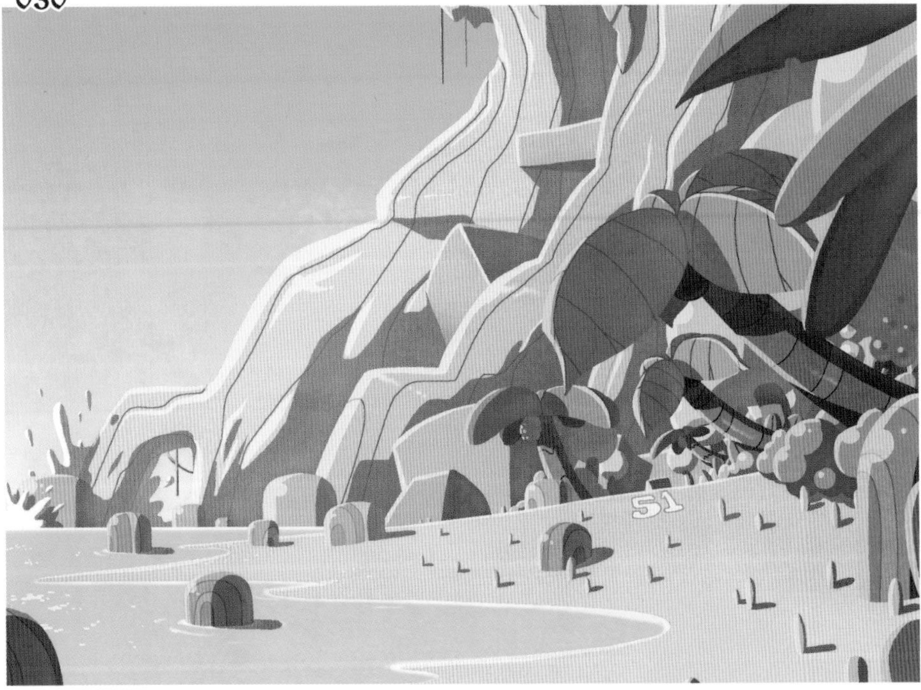
51

031

Well done. You find another gold piece! Now, go to 56.

032

135
306

033

341
9

034

296
91

035

You're going to have to leave your boat here to continue on.
163 →

036

25 →

037

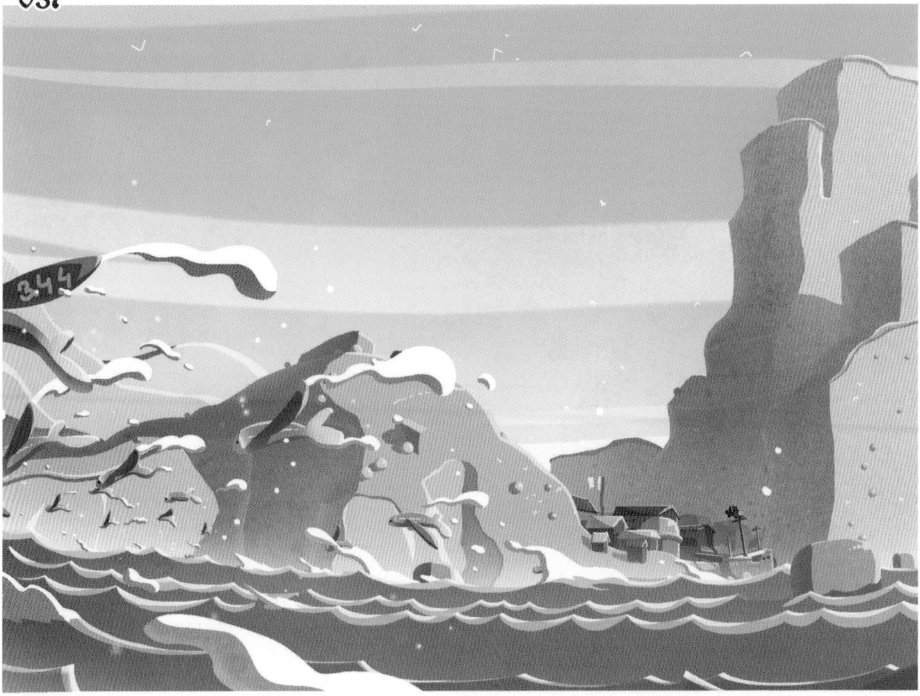
344

038

WOW, THANKS! I'VE BEEN STUMPED FOR THREE WEEKS NOW! TO SHOW MY GRATITUDE, PLEASE COME TO MY PLACE AT 260 AND ENJOY SOME DRIED SHRIMP JUICE.
You can also kindly decline his offer, then leave to 292.

039

305

040

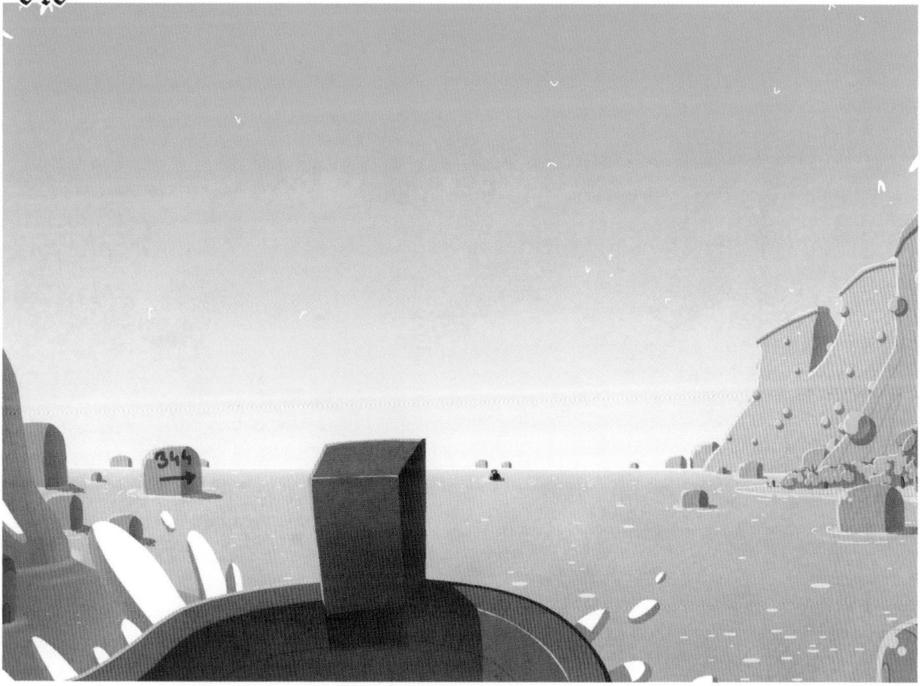
344

041

91

042

234
61
THE LAST ADVENTURER WHO VISITED US DECIDED TO SETTLE HERE.

043

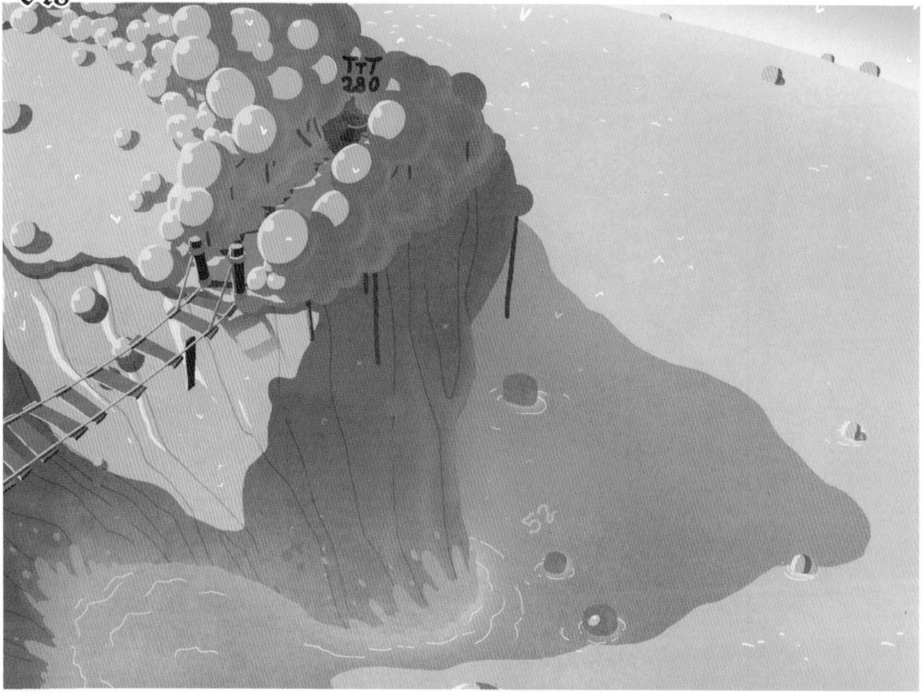
280
52

044

AH, AH, IN MY ARMS, MY FRIEND! HERE, TAKE THIS RING. YOU DESERVE IT! IT WILL MAKE YOU EVEN SMARTER.
The pirate offers you a ring. It's as light as a feather and grants you 2 additional Intelligence points permanently. Now, return to 115 and do not come back to the boat. The pirate you just finished humiliating would not appreciate a return visit.

045

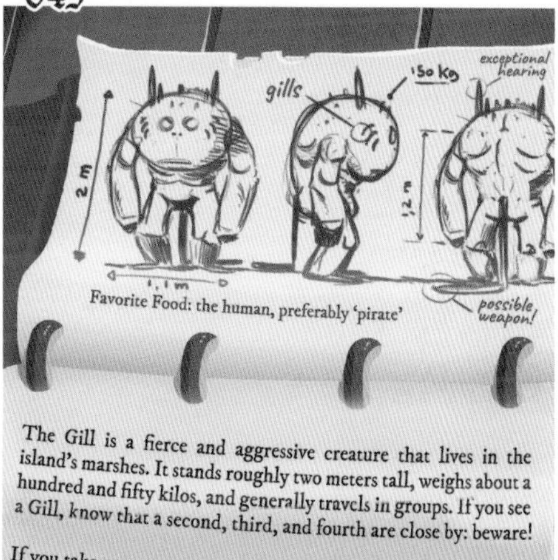
gills
150 kg
exceptional hearing
2 m
Favorite Food: the human, preferably 'pirate'
possible weapon!
The Gill is a fierce and aggressive creature that lives in the island's marshes. It stands roughly two meters tall, weighs about a hundred and fifty kilos, and generally travels in groups. If you see a Gill, know that a second, third, and fourth are close by: beware!
If you take care not to act surprised or scared, you can overcome them without much trouble by hitting them hard in the knee or the glottis.
P. S. a little secret: each Gill carries a gold with him. Each Gill you kill is another gold piece in your bag!
Wow, bravo! You know how to fight Gills now! Now, return to the frame you came from.

046

301

047

Despite your proficiency at slaughtering Gills, you'll only be able to get past them if you have at least 10 Agility. If so, make quick work of them and head to 318. Otherwise, you'll need to run away to 255.

048

86

049

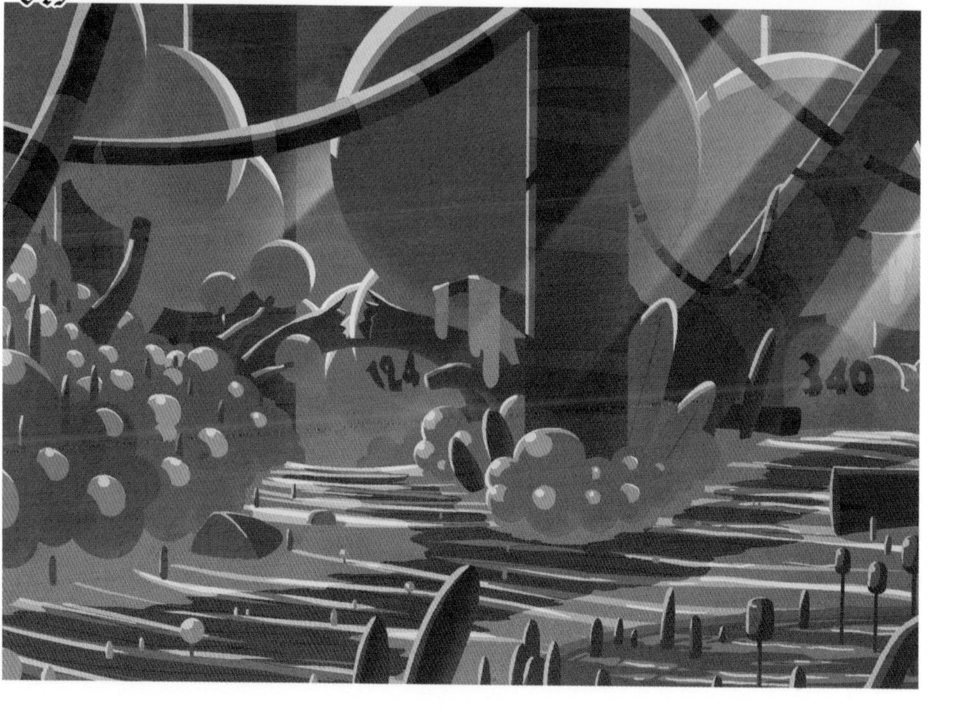
124
340

050

78
334

051

252
276

Very nice dive, bravo! However, if you have fewer than 13 Agility, you're dead from the impact. You can, of course, begin your adventure anew at 1.
329
150

053

HMM, NO, THAT DOESN'T RING A BELL. BUT GO ASK GUILLAM. IF ANYONE SAW YOUR MAN, IT'S HIM! YOU'LL USUALLY FIND HIM NEAR TOWN. NOW GET OUT OF HERE TO 115 BEFORE MY PARROT EATS YOUR EYES OUT.
The captain does not wish to see you again. You are no longer welcome to visit 64.

054

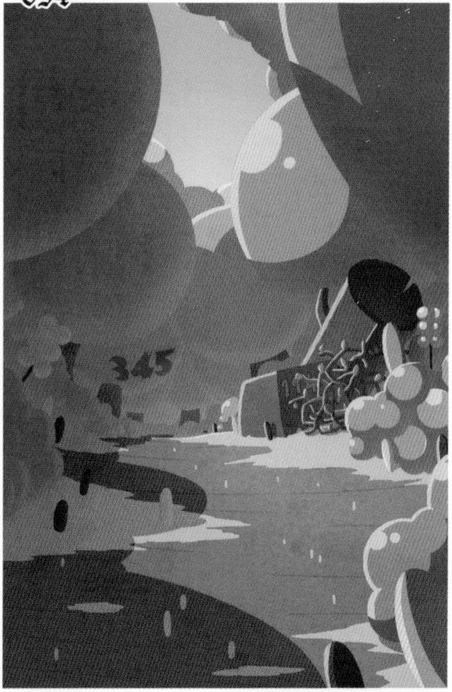
345

055

YEAH, I SAW HIM. AND MARK MY WORDS, IF I CATCH HIM, HE'LL BE SORRY! LOOK AT WHAT HE DID TO MY BANANA!
You should leave to 175 before this monkey goes bananas.

056

47
255

057

If you're done enjoying the view, you can return to 6.

058

You should get out of here before you drown! Return to 28.

059

OH YES! YOU DEFINITELY WANT TO FIND HIM, MY BOY! GO CHECK OUT THE EDGE OF THE SWAMP. IF YOU'RE QUICK, YOU'LL DEFINITELY FIND HIM.
You can go immediately to 343, or you could instead take some time to reflect, and return to 28.

060

259

061

←42
63→

062

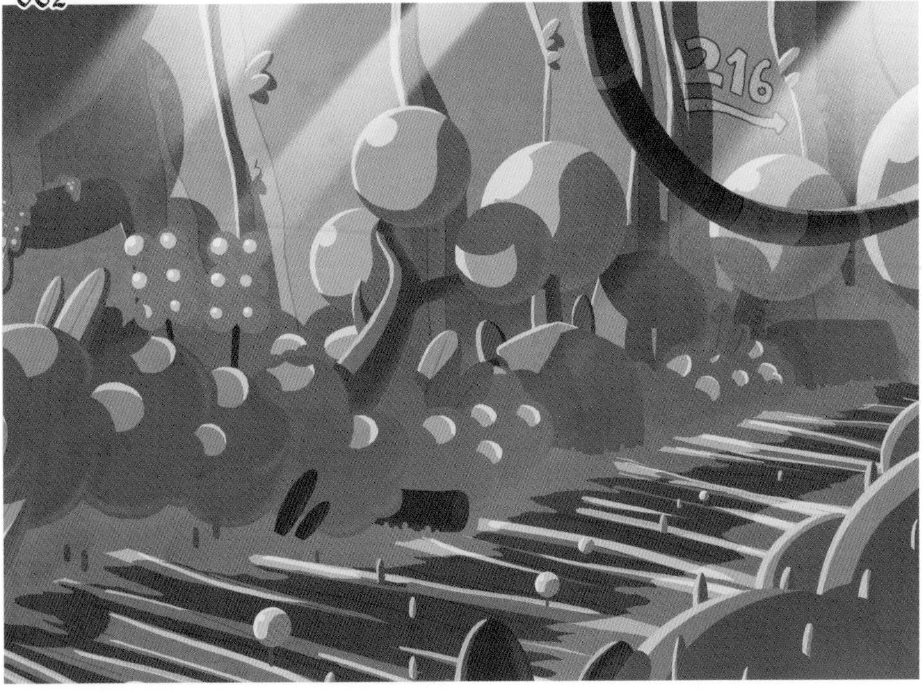
216

063

304
61

064

WHAT'RE YOU DOING THERE, SHRIMP? YOU GET THE IMPRESSION THAT WE'RE HAVING A DOORS OPEN DAY OR WHAT?
To find out whether or not you can visit his ship, go to 241. To ask him if he's seen the person you're looking for, go to 53. If you'd rather turn back, go to 115.

065

170

066

204

067

102

068

291
225

069

Unfortunately, you've been crushed by a four ton stone.
You can always start again at 1.
BIG TRAP THAT HURTS YOU

070

245
286
89

071

148
DK

072

If you have at least 10 Agility,
you can try to jump to 88.
88
278 →

073

I don't know if it was your keen observations skills that saved you or what,
but you managed to escape a terrible Gill that would've eaten you in a bite.
50

074

261
289
115
199
185
LIBRARY

075

IT'S BEEN AGES SINCE I'VE CROSSED PATHS WITH ANYONE! THINGS HAVEN'T BEEN EASY LIVING HERE. HA HA!
ANYWAYS, TELL ME, DO YOU HAVE ANY FLOWER BULBS TO SPARE? MY LITTLE KITTY LOVES THEM!
To know more about these famous flower bulbs, head to 256.
Otherwise, turn back to 32.

076

198

077

215

078

99

079

There's still time to turn back to 107. Maybe he'll come back.
287

080

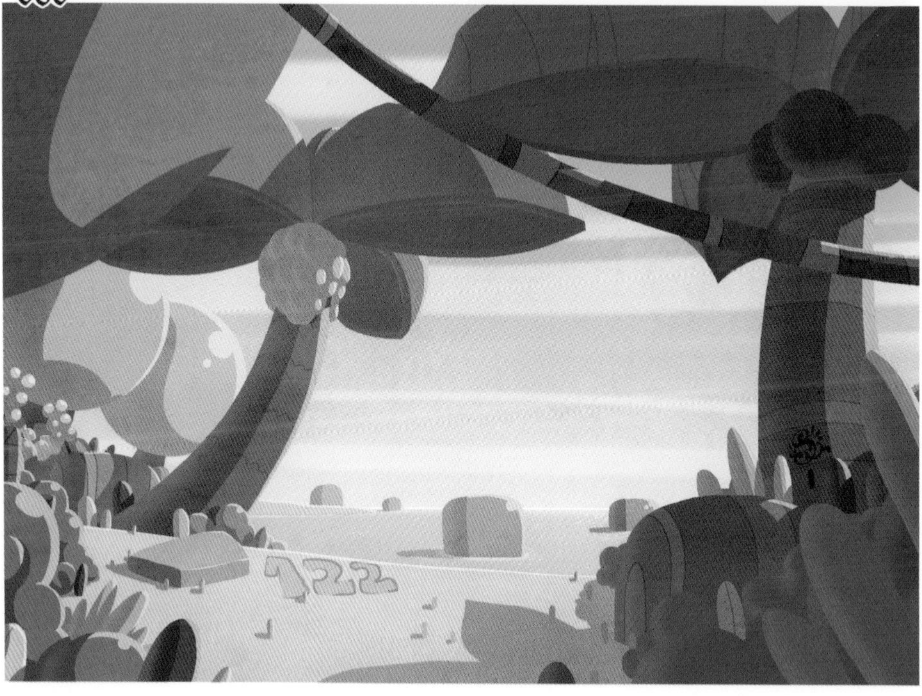
122

081

123

082

Count the number of turns necessary to arrive at the center, multiply that number by 10 and go to the corresponding frame.
WIN

083

084

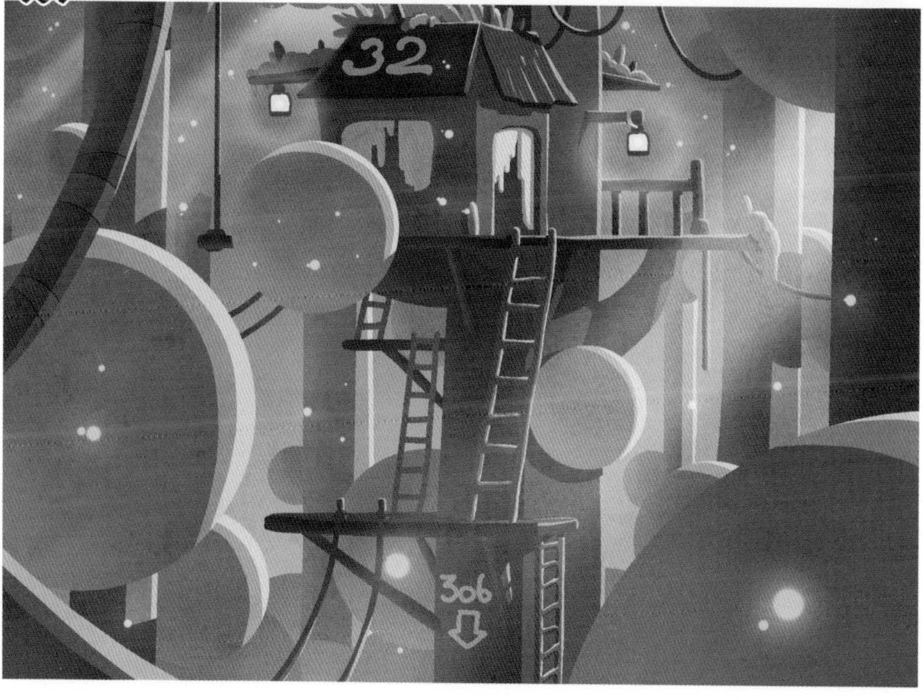
32
306

085

41

086

You can turn around and go to 340.

087

Unless you're hoping to make a nice omelette, or become one, I would recommend you run away to 214, and quickly!

088

94
120

089

Unfortunately, you chose the wrong vine. An itsy bitsy 4 ton rock flattened you pretty good. You can begin your adventure again at 1.
BIG TRAP THAT HURTS YOU

090

220
225

091

273
236

092

WHAT ARE YOU DOING HERE, PIG?
If you wish to respond, head over to 349.
If you'd prefer to escape, there's still time to go to 23.
If you'd like to fight them using Strength (minimum 10 Strength), go to 132.
If you'd like to fight them using Agility (minimum 10 Agility), go to 118.

093

You head to 172 at full speed and can't return, or you may decide to engage this... seagull in conversation. In which case, go to 98.

094

265

095

267

096

YOU SEE, YOUNG ADVENTURER, THIS AMULET IS QUITE EXCEPTIONAL. IF YOU WEAR IT, YOU WILL BECOME MORE AGILE (+2 POINTS), AND YOU WILL ALSO HAVE THE POWER TO REPEL THE LIVING DEAD, WHO WILL NEVER DARE FIGHT YOU. IT IS YOURS, IN EXCHANGE FOR A STRAWBERRY, A RUBY, A PINK LEAF, AND A VIAL OF SERPENT VENOM. IF YOU POSSESS THESE OBJECTS, TAKE THE AMULET AND GO TO 353.
Note this frame's number (96) on your character sheet. You can return here whenever you find the required objects. Now, go to 353.

097

214
136

098

YES? WHY ARE YOU SQUAWKING AT ME?
If you'd like to ask her questions about the fugitive, go to 202.
If you'd like to admire the landscape, go to 130.
If you'd prefer to turn back, go to 172.

099

217

100

82
11

101

353

102

49

103

313

104

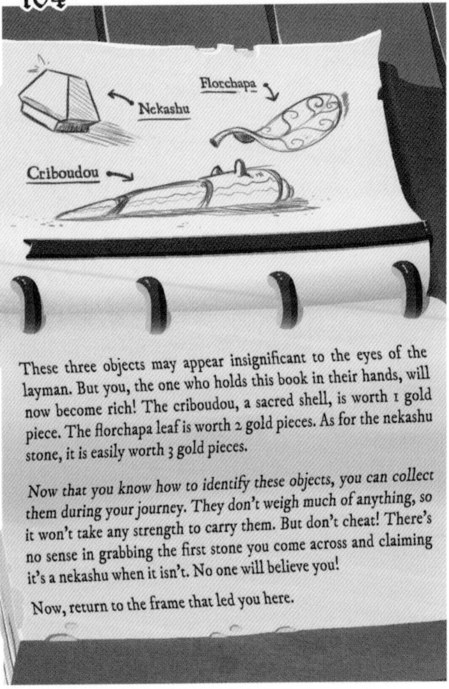
Florchapa
Nekashu
Criboudou
These three objects may appear insignificant to the eyes of the layman. But you, the one who holds this book in their hands, will now become rich! The criboudou, a sacred shell, is worth 1 gold piece. The florchapa leaf is worth 2 gold pieces. As for the nekashu stone, it is easily worth 3 gold pieces.
Now that you know how to identify these objects, you can collect them during your journey. They don't weigh much of anything, so it won't take any strength to carry them. But don't cheat! There's no sense in grabbing the first stone you come across and claiming it's a nekashu when it isn't. No one will believe you!
Now, return to the frame that led you here.

105

There's still time to turn back.
To do so, go to 172.
231

106

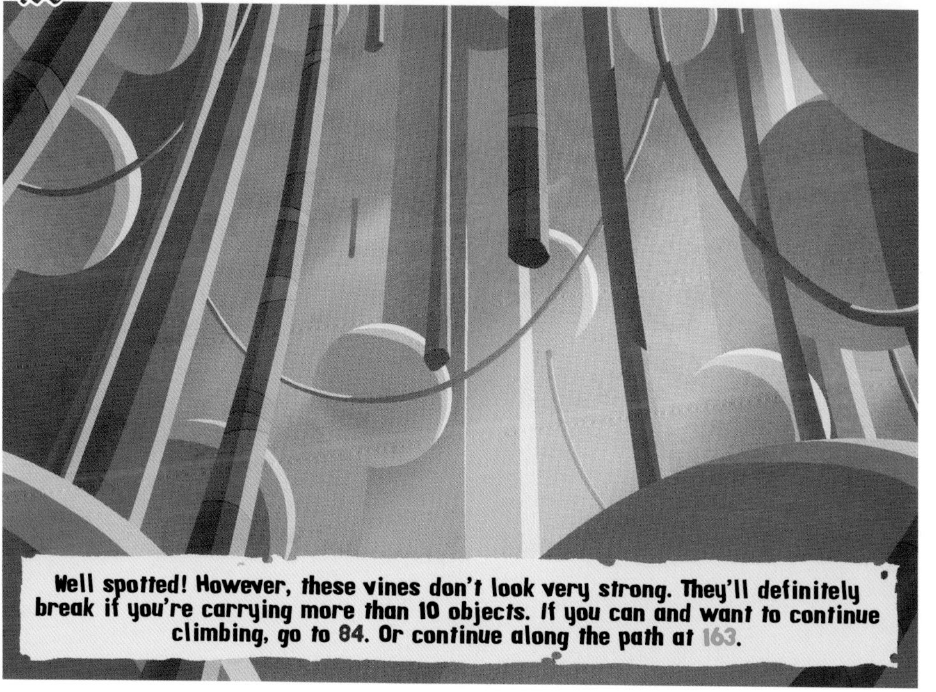
Well spotted! However, these vines don't look very strong. They'll definitely break if you're carrying more than 10 objects. If you can and want to continue climbing, go to 84. Or continue along the path at 163.

107

347

108

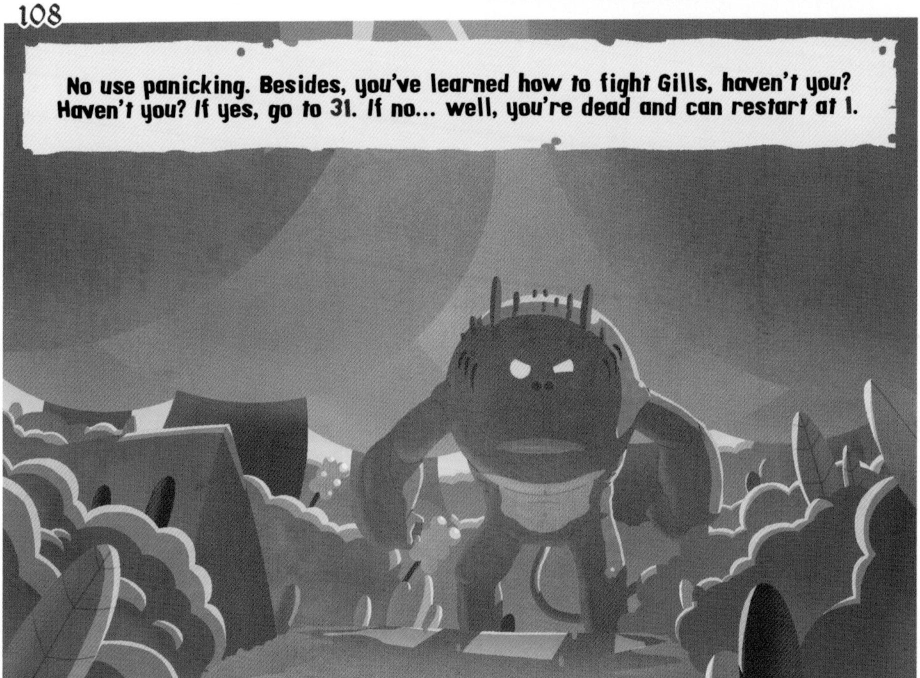
No use panicking. Besides, you've learned how to fight Gills, haven't you? Haven't you? If yes, go to 31. If no... well, you're dead and can restart at 1.

109

SHOP
I
MUUT
15

110

13

111

↓ 326 ↓

112

238

113

201

114

You found a secret passage, well spotted! If you have at least 10 Strength, you can crawl through the brambles to 3. If not, don't bother trying. Just turn yourself back around to 54.

115

325
64
144
34

116

Take whatever you like and go to 181.

117

217
113
162

118

WELL THAT WAS QUICK.
YEAH... THEY WERE WEAK AS A KITTEN. PRETTY FUNNY!
Um... yeah... you're quick on your toes, but without weapons or any brute Strength, it doesn't mean much in a fight. You can start your adventure over at 1.

119

271→

120

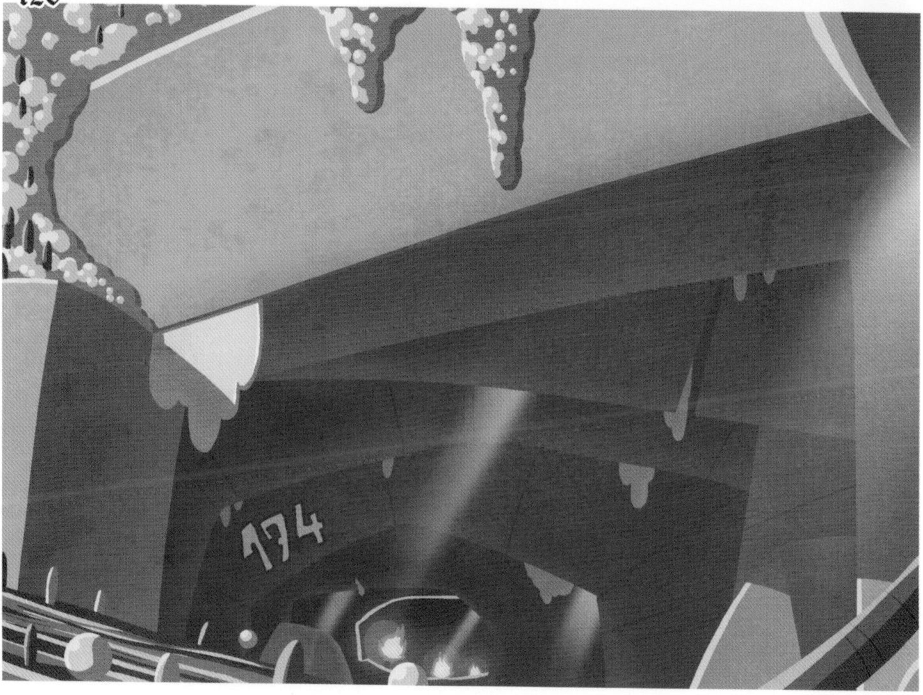
174

121

ANY SPARE CHANGE?
126
112

122

36

123

189
292

124

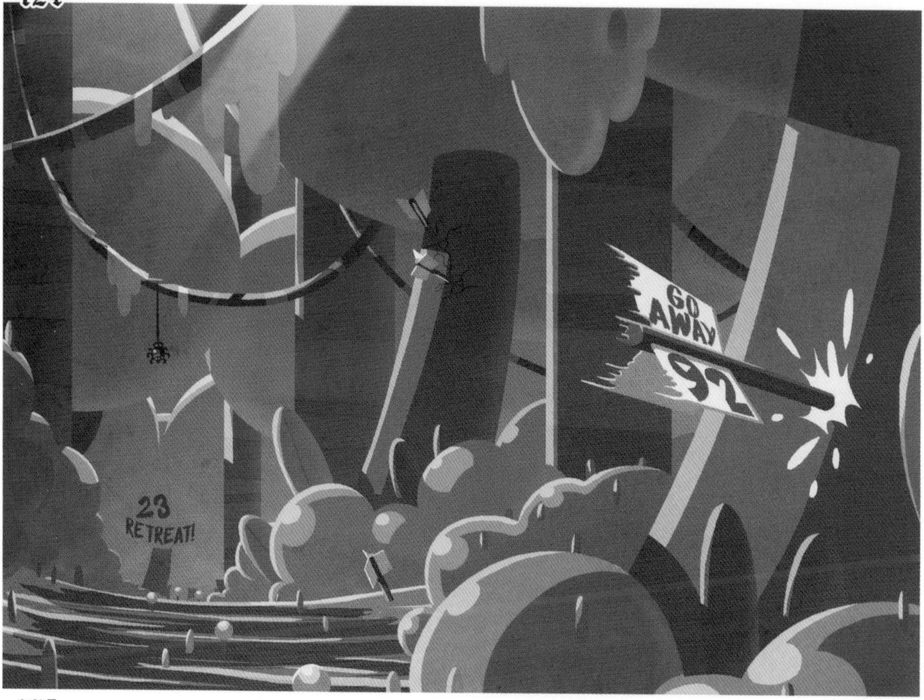
GO AWAY
92
23
RETREAT!

125

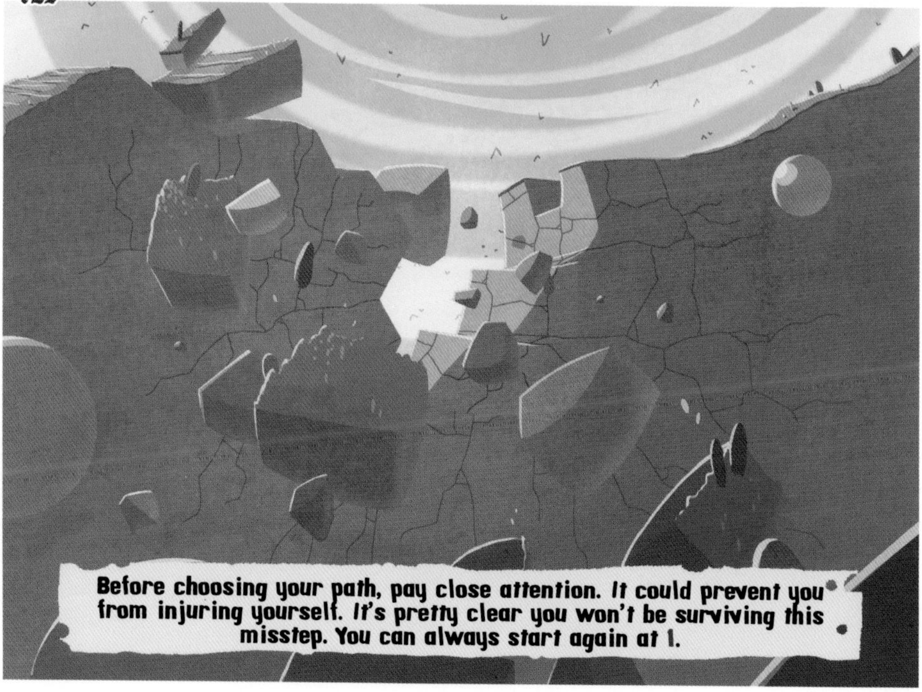
Before choosing your path, pay close attention. It could prevent you from injuring yourself. It's pretty clear you won't be surviving this misstep. You can always start again at 1.

126

WHAT? YOU AIN'T GOT NOTHIN' FOR ME? THEN GET OUTTA HERE BEFORE GUILLAM GIVES YA A SLAP!
You would probably do well to turn back to 112 before this beggar gives you... something to remember him by. Unless, that is, his name means something to you. In which case, go to 146.

127

HEY, YOU THERE! IF YOU KNOW HOW TO PLAY CHESS, HELP ME WIN THIS GAME IN TWO MOVES. OTHERWISE, LEAVE US ALONE AND GO BACK TO 6.
Game on! The numbers of the pieces, side by side and in the order of movement, that you need to move to place your opponent in checkmate, will form a two digit number. That number will tell you which frame to go to. If you go to the correct frame, the man with the mohawk will be very pleased with you!

128

254

129

You gain 5 gold pieces for the right answer. Now, continue your adventure at 240.

Beautiful view, eh? Okay, enough lollygagging. Back to 98.

131

35

132

268

133

GREETINGS, NOBLE ADVENTURER! PLEASE COME IN! A LITTLE COMPANY'LL DO ME GOOD.
There's still time to turn around back to 32. Otherwise, go to 75.

134

40

135

Mystery
SHERLOCK HOLMES
Too bad! If you'd arrived two seconds earlier, you could have walked away with a complete collection of Graphic Novel Adventures. Maybe next time!

136

106
163

137

239

138

Again?! How many time do I have to tell you to look before you leap? Your boat is destroyed and you... well you're dead, obviously. Get started again at 1.

139

ENTER, VOYAGER. I'VE BEEN WAITING FOR YOU!
A little dark in here, don't you think? If this place gives you the heebie jeebies, you can head back to 22. Otherwise, stick around at 219.

140

Oh great, a corn maze. It's funny when you're ten years old. Not so much when you're trying to find someone. Head back whence you came at 28.

141

119

142

THE BAG, SCOUNDREL! HAND IT OVER. NOW!

If you have at least 14 Agility or 14 Strength and you own a weapon, go to 149.
If you have at least 14 Intelligence, go to 206.
Otherwise, go to 352.

143

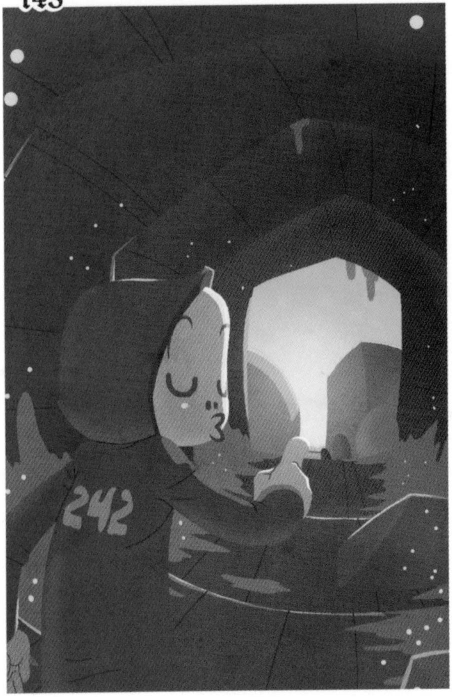
242

144

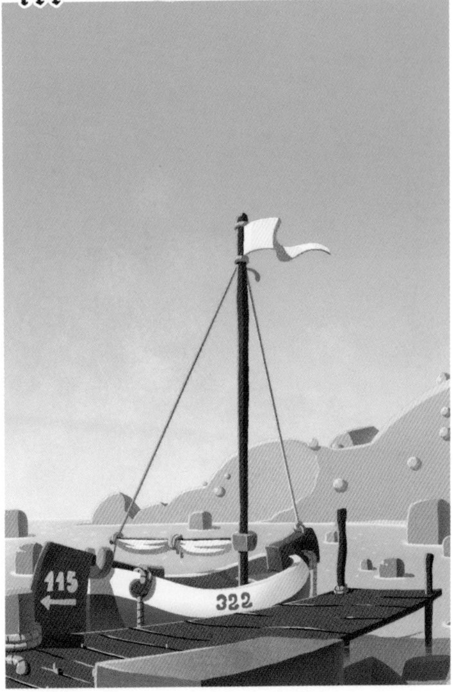
115
322

145

YOU KNOW THAT JERK? HE TRAMPLED MY LETTUCE AND CRUSHED MY CABBAGE! IF I CATCH HIM, I'LL WRING HIS NECK! HE HEADED TOWARDS THE CITY OF SKULLS, NORTH-EAST OF HERE. IT'S LUCKY FOR HIM THAT I'M SCARED OF THE CITY.
A precious clue! Your fugitive is headed towards the island's fortified city. It's not exactly close, but at least you know which way he's headed. Hit the road to 76 on the double.

146

YEAH, THE NAME'S GUILLAM, AND...? WHAT? WHO TOLD YOU ABOUT ME? WHO? CHICO? PABLO? RICO? BE CAREFUL WHAT YOU SAY NOW, BECAUSE HEARING TWO OF THOSE NAMES GETS MY BLOOD BOILIN'.
Alright, do not answer unless you are certain, otherwise you could end up paying dearly! If you'd rather not take the risk, leave to 112. To answer him, go to 316.

147

148

193

149

Well played! Now, head on over to 288.

150

The lack of oxygen is starting to become a problem. You can take 10 objects of your choice. The gold pieces weigh nothing, but everything else weighs 1 each. Then, head quickly to the surface and go to 329.

151

What, come on! The number of heads lying around didn't give you any pause? You're dead, torn apart by the crows. You can restart at 1.

152

YOU HAVE DONE WELL, VOYAGER. LEAVE THE VILLAGE IMMEDIATELY VIA THE PORT, TRAVEL ALONG THE COAST AND DISEMBARK WHEN YOU ARE REQUIRED TO DO SO. SEARCH WELL: YOU WILL FIND A PASSAGE. SINK INTO THE DARK FOREST AND ADD 47 TO THE NUMBER OF LINES YOU SEE UNDER THIS SYMBOL.
GO, LEAVE QUICKLY TO 22.

153

134

154

THE ANSWER WAS "NIGHT" OR "KNIGHTS", OBVIOUSLY. HA HA HA!
If you got the right answer, the guard lets you in and you can proceed to 74. Otherwise, continue on your way to 61.

155

265

156

294

157

Ha ha! You showed him! Who's the clever one now? Pick up the 5 gold pieces around his body and return to 350.

158

NO, I HAVEN'T SEEN YOUR FRIEND AROUND HERE. I'LL BE FRANK WITH YA. EVEN IF I HAD, I WOULDN'T TELL YA. NOW, GET OUTTA MY BAR: WE DON'T LIKE YOUR KIND AROUND HERE.
And there you have it. Your gut was right about the barkeep after all: he's not very pleasant! Return to 74.

159

This part of the swamp is difficult to access. Unless you have winged boots, you should probably turn around. Up to you! To continue, go to 192. If you'd prefer to turn around, return to 217.

160

141

161

CORSAIR
forty five
Nothing much in this dump!
Head to the swamp at 294.

162

163

306

164

OH, THAT? IT'S NOTHING... JUST A GUY WHO CAME BY THIS MORNING TO ASK ME HOW HE COULD GET TO THE CITY. I INVITED HIM TO JOIN ME FOR A GLASS OF SHRIMP JUICE. WHEN MY GLUTTONOUS CAT WENT OVER TO HIM, THE MAN PET MY CAT AND TURNED HIM TO GOLD.
ANY SUGAR?
Curious story... Finish your delicious beverage and go to 292.

165

GRRRR... WHAT DO YOU WANT?
If you'd like to ask him a question about the person you're looking for, go to 145. If you'd prefer to ask him questions about him and his brothers, go to 177.

166

237

167

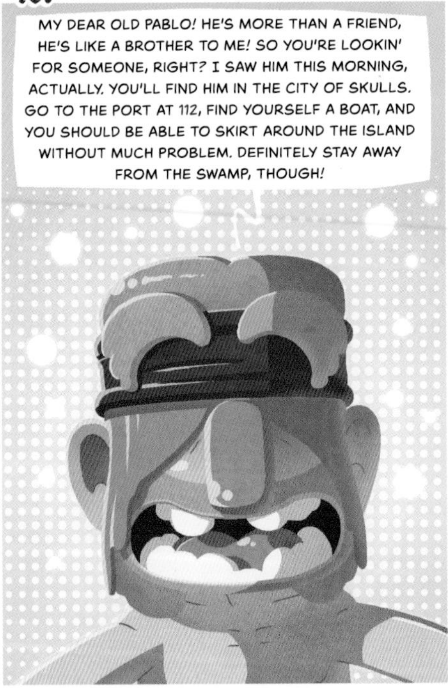
MY DEAR OLD PABLO! HE'S MORE THAN A FRIEND, HE'S LIKE A BROTHER TO ME! SO YOU'RE LOOKIN' FOR SOMEONE, RIGHT? I SAW HIM THIS MORNING, ACTUALLY. YOU'LL FIND HIM IN THE CITY OF SKULLS. GO TO THE PORT AT 112, FIND YOURSELF A BOAT, AND YOU SHOULD BE ABLE TO SKIRT AROUND THE ISLAND WITHOUT MUCH PROBLEM. DEFINITELY STAY AWAY FROM THE SWAMP, THOUGH!

168

123
61

169

115

170

117

171

Listen, I get it. You want to fight them to show how brave you are... but i'm gonna have to go ahead and recommend you leave to 303 before these ferocious creatures eat you alive. Sound good?

172

Summit : 125
Village : 230
Hector :
105

173

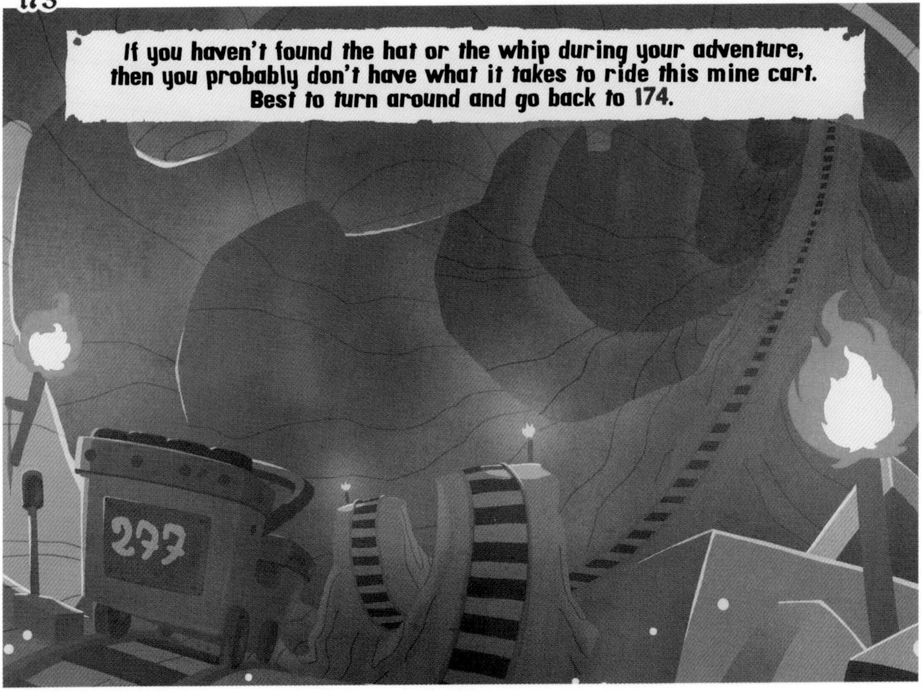
If you haven't found the hat or the whip during your adventure, then you probably don't have what it takes to ride this mine cart. Best to turn around and go back to 174.
273

174

300
173

175

109
315
212

176

US? WHY, WE LIVE HERE, AWAY FROM ALL THE CONFLICTS, THIEVES, PROWLERS, AND OTHER EVIL CREATURES. NOW AND THEN WE DO SOME TRADING WITH THE BANDITS IN THE NEARBY VILLAGE. WE GET ALONG WELL.
If you'd like to know more about the village of bandits, head to 317. If you'd like to trade with the Thanaton, head to 333. If you'd prefer to leave the cave, go to 330.

177

GET OUT OF MY FIELD! I'VE GOT NOTHING TO SAY TO YOU.
This charming gentleman is quite clearly not in the mood to discuss the latest in philosophical literature. Return to 28.

178

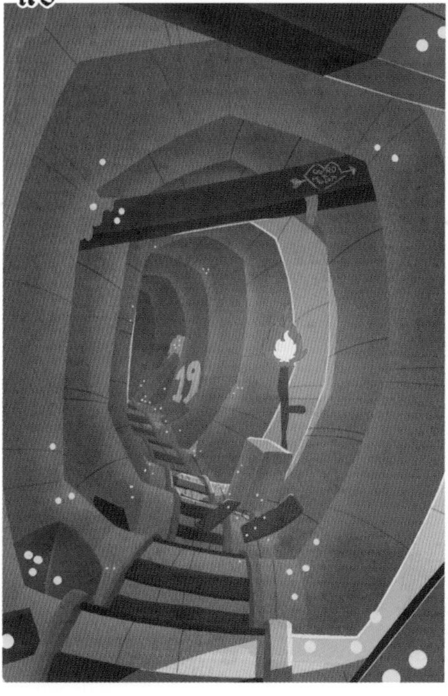
19

179

73
108

180

I told you: bananas are useful! You're dead and can restart your adventure at 1.

181

182

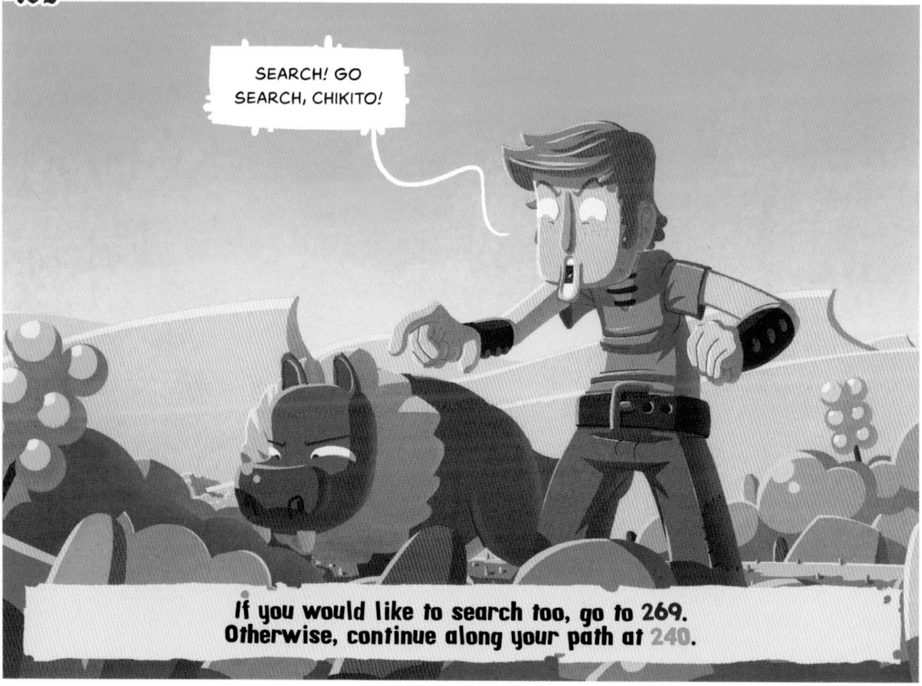
SEARCH! GO SEARCH, CHIKITO!
If you would like to search too, go to 269. Otherwise, continue along your path at 240.

183

62

184

WE CAN TELL THAT YOU ARE BRAVE: MANY HAVE TRIED TO DESCEND THE ROPE AND LEFT WITH BROKEN TEETH... AND BONES.
WHAT BRINGS YOU HERE?
If you would like to recount your story and ask for help regarding the man you seek, go to 332. If you would like, you could also interrogate the Thanatons about their community at 176.

185

G'DAY, STRANGER. DO ANY OF THESE ITEMS INTEREST YOU? EACH OF THESE BOOKS COSTS EITHER 1 FEATHER, 1 MAGNIFYING GLASS, OR 3 GOLD PIECES. YOU CAN PUT IT IN YOUR BAG NOW AND START USING IT IMMEDIATELY. PLUS, THESE BOOKS DON'T EVEN WEIGH MUCH OF ANYTHING!
How to Find Gold in 3 Easy Lessons
104
+1 in the characteristic of your choice
Monsters For Dummies
45
Once you've finished shopping, go to 74.

186

I SAW YOUR FUGITIVE, MOST CERTAINLY! HE EVEN ASKED ME FOR SOME BREAD AND WATER. A REAL NICE CHAP. SO YOU CAN BE DARN SURE THAT I WON'T BE TELLING YOU ANYTHING ABOUT HIM. THAT IS, UNLESS YOU HAVE A GOLD PIECE TO OFFER ME?
Go to 59 if you have the gold piece to pay the man. Otherwise, head back to 28.

187

74
223

188

249

189

If you'd like to speak to this man, go to 246.
Otherwise, leave to 292 before he sees you.

190

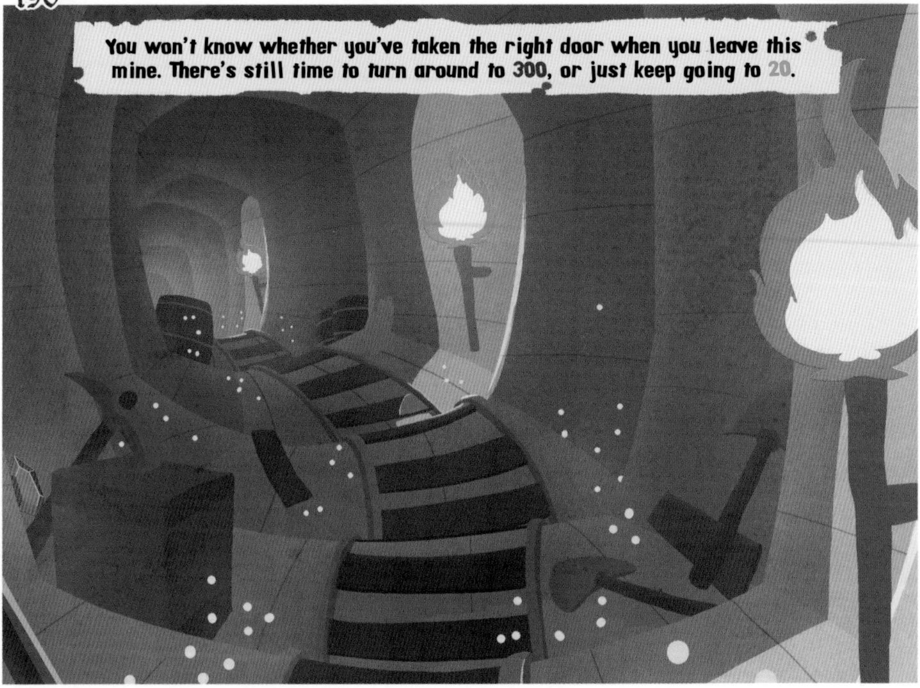
You won't know whether you've taken the right door when you leave this mine. There's still time to turn around to 300, or just keep going to 20.

191

WHAT CAN I DO FOR YOU, FRIEND?
If you'd like to ask him a question about the man you're searching for, go to 186. If you'd like to interrogate him about his brothers, go to 314.

192

For crying out loud! You're such a liar! Without the magical item in your possession, you wind up dead, and for good reason! Feel free to start again at 1.

193

Alright? What now? You could head towards the guards, but they don't seem all that accommodating. You could also just turn around and head back to 326. However, if you do, the long journey back will reduce your Strength by 1 point (and you'll be forced to throw out an item if your bag is full).
196

194

2↗
101
346→

195

264

196

Quick! If you have a banana, give it to them and go to 128. Otherwise, you're just going to have to turn around and head to 326... that journey will exhaust you, however, and you will lose a Strength point (as well as an object, if your bag is full).

197

271

198

83

199

YOU, GOOD SIR, LOOK LIKE AN ADVENTURER. TELL ME, WOULD YOU HAPPEN TO HAVE 5 STRAWBERRIES? I NEED SOME FOR A FISH SOUP I'M MAKING. I'LL GIVE YOU 10 GOLD PIECES.
AN'S FRIEND
If you have 5 strawberries to sell, remove them for your list and gain 10 gold pieces. Return to 74.

200

HEY NOW... DON'T GO TAKING ME FOR A LLAMA NOW...! BY THE LOOKS OF YOU, I DOUBT YOU HAVE 200 GOLD PIECES TO YOUR NAME. SO YOU CAN TAKE YOUR RIDICULOUS SCARF, YOUR SWORD, AND YOUR BIG MUSCLES AND GET LOST TO 353. SCRAM!

201

188

202

HMMM. YES, I VAGUELY REMEMBER... I BELIEVE HE WANTED TO GO TO THE CITY OF SKULLS, BUT I CAN'T SAY WHETHER OR NOT HE MADE IT... WANNA KNOW ANYTHING ELSE?
If you'd like to admire the view, go to 130. To turn around, go to 172. To ask the seagull for help leaving this place, go to 342.

203

HAVE YOU FOUND MY RING IN THIS HERE CORN FIELD? I'VE BEEN LOOKING FOR WEEKS!
If you've found the ring and want to hand it over, head to 281. If you haven't seen it or just want to hold onto it, go to 58.

204

169

205

WE FOUND THIS ON THE BEACH. CAN YOU TELL ME WHAT IT IS?
If you have at least 13 Intelligence, you can read it more clearly at 309. if you're unable to solve the puzzle, return to 175.

206

OH, LOOK OVER THERE!

Very clever! They didn't see *that* one coming! Now, run to 288.

207

TREE TOP TOWN
43

You're probably wondering what the Thanatons are pointing at. Well, it's you. Pretty high, huh? Know that you can get to the village - like any good Thanaton would - by climbing the rope to 184. It's no use to tell you that if you fall your neck will snap like a pencil. You could also just choose to leave the poor Thanatons alone and continue along your path to 21.

209

Phew! Nice getaway! Catch your breath, and choose a (better) path forward. Would you like to visit the charming little village you see before you in 42 or would you prefer to keep on your path to 172?

210

351

211

You should really revisit your flying lessons, but all in all, not too shabby. Get yourself out of this tree and head to 42.

212

LOVELY! IT'S NOT EVERY DAY I GET A VISITOR! WHAT CAN I DO FOR YOU, FRIEND?
To ask him if he's seen your fugitive, go to 55. If you're not comfortable with the fact that you'd be conversing with a monkey - all in all, a little weird - go to 175.

213

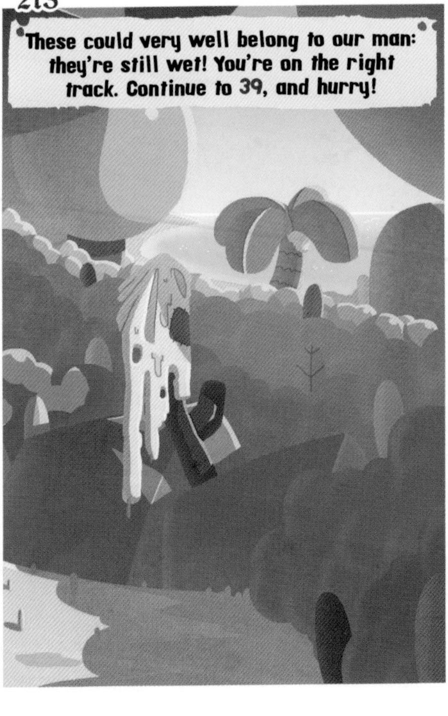
These could very well belong to our man: they're still wet! You're on the right track. Continue to 39, and hurry!

214

68

215

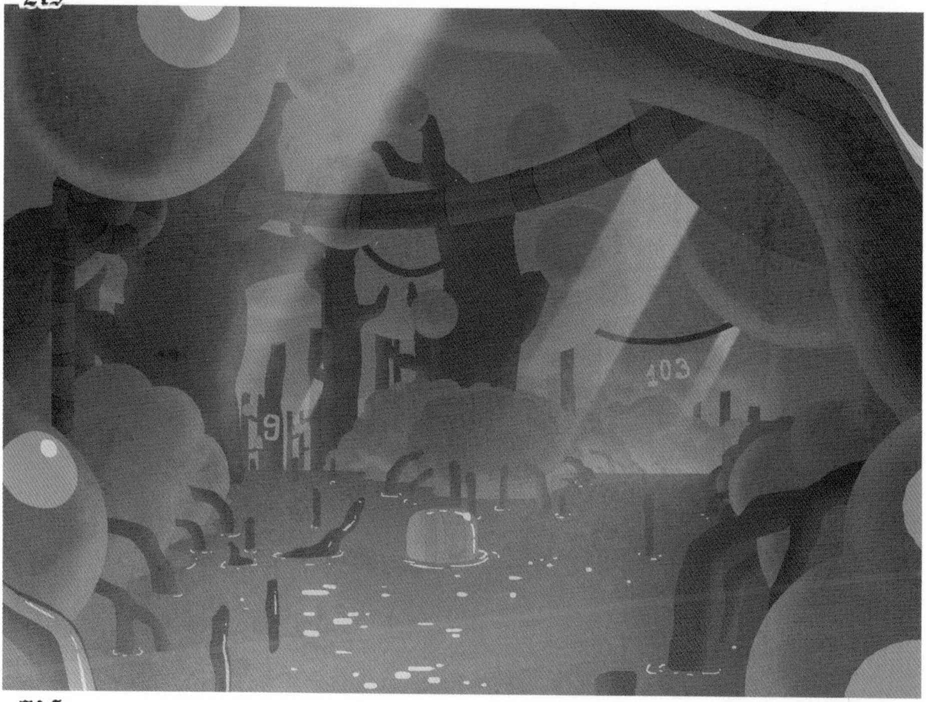
9
103

216

72

217

159
54

218

228
324

219

NOT A WORD, TRAVELER! I KNOW EXACTLY WHY YOU'RE HERE. GIVE ME A GOLD PIECE AND I'LL GIVE YOU VALUABLE INFORMATION.
Up to you. If you'd like to hear what the seer has to say, go to 152. If not, turn yourself around and go to 22.

220

331

221

A SCARECROW? GOODNESS ME, WHY DIDN'T I THINK OF THAT? HA, HA, WELL PLAYED, STRANGER! PLEASE, TAKE ONE OF THESE 3 BRACELETS. I HAVE NO IDEA WHAT THEY'RE GOOD FOR, BUT I'M SURE THEY'LL COME IN HANDY.
If you chose the blue bracelet, add one Strength point to your sheet; if yellow, one Agility point; and if red, one Intelligence point. The bracelet is a light object and doesn't weigh much. Obviously, if "scarecrow" wasn't your answer, Mistral doesn't offer you anything and you can return to 28.

222

100

223

< 187
29 >

224

I WOULDN'T DARE FIGHT A HERO OF YOUR CALIBER: TAKE THESE FEATHERS AND MY GOLD COOL LORD CLUB CARD. HEAD BACK TO THE CITY AT 336.
COOL LORD CLUB

225

291
302

226

319

227

WELL DONE! I WOULD NEVER HAVE BELIEVED YOU WERE SO SMART! NOW, AS I AM A MAN OF MY WORD, I WILL TELL YOU THAT YOUR FRIEND SEEMED TO BE HEADING FOR THE CITY OF SKULLS, AT THE EAST OF THE ISLAND. AND, SEEING AS HOW YOU'VE IMPRESSED ME, I WANT TO OFFER YOU THIS HELMET.
GO ON, AND NO NEED TO THANK ME! THIS HELMET IS BASICALLY WORTHLESS. NOW HEAD TO 253 AND FIND YOUR FRIEND.
STRENGTH

228

350
298
324

229

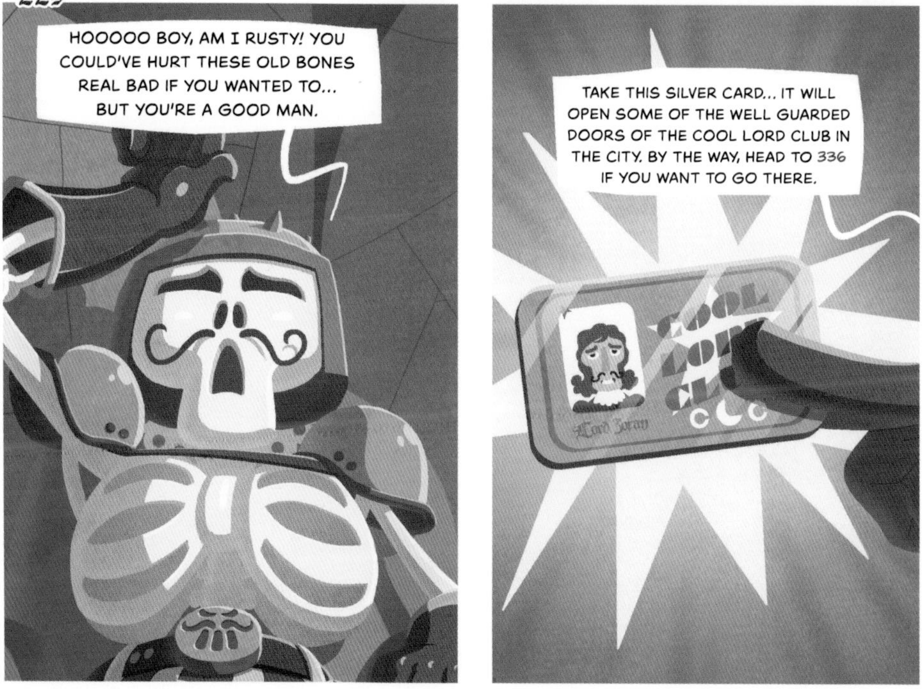
HOOOOO BOY, AM I RUSTY! YOU COULD'VE HURT THESE OLD BONES REAL BAD IF YOU WANTED TO... BUT YOU'RE A GOOD MAN.
TAKE THIS SILVER CARD... IT WILL OPEN SOME OF THE WELL GUARDED DOORS OF THE COOL LORD CLUB IN THE CITY. BY THE WAY, HEAD TO 336 IF YOU WANT TO GO THERE.

230

2

231

There's still time to run away: go to 172.

232

NOT SO CLEVER
NOW, ARE YOU?
He's right about that, you're dead now.
Restart your adventure at 1.

233

Oof... well played! But you lose 1 Strength point due to exhaustion. Decrease your Strength on your character sheet and, if your bag is full, drop an object, too.

234

WHERE DO YOU THINK YOU'RE GOING? NO ONE PASSES THIS WAY WITHOUT SOLVING THE SACRED RIDDLE.

AND WOULDN'T YOU KNOW, I'M THE ONE WHO WROTE THE RIDDLE. IT'S YOUR LUCKY DAY! LISTEN: "YOU CAN FIND ME SURROUNDING A SHINING MOON, OR INSIDE SHINING ARMOR. WHAT AM I?"
To give your answer, go to 154.

235

70
69

236

Good eye! That snake could have killed you! Extract some of its venom.
It may come in handy later. Then go to 194.

237

65

238

22

239

179

240

249

241

LISTEN HERE, JOKER. YOU'RE GONNA TAKE YOUR CLICKS AND CLACKS AND LEAVE. NOW! THE ONLY THING THAT COULD MAKE ME CHANGE MY MIND WOULD BE A SACK OF 10 GOLD COINS. IF NOT, SCRAM!
If you have 10 gold pieces and you're willing to give them to the captain, you go to 6. If not, turn back to 115, and never return here.

242

AND HERE WE ARE IN THE FRESH AIR, ADVENTURER! JUST FOLLOW THIS LITTLE PATH TO ARRIVE AT THE VILLAGE ENTRANCE IN 42. YOU SHOULD BE ABLE TO ANSWER OLAF'S RIDDLE WITHOUT TOO MUCH TROUBLE. BEST OF LUCK, MY FRIEND!

243

To go to 12, climb to the top of these trees like a little monkey. Collect as many bananas as you can on your way up. They don't weigh anything and they might come in handy. However, you can only ever climb up, and can only cross each branch once.

244

50

245

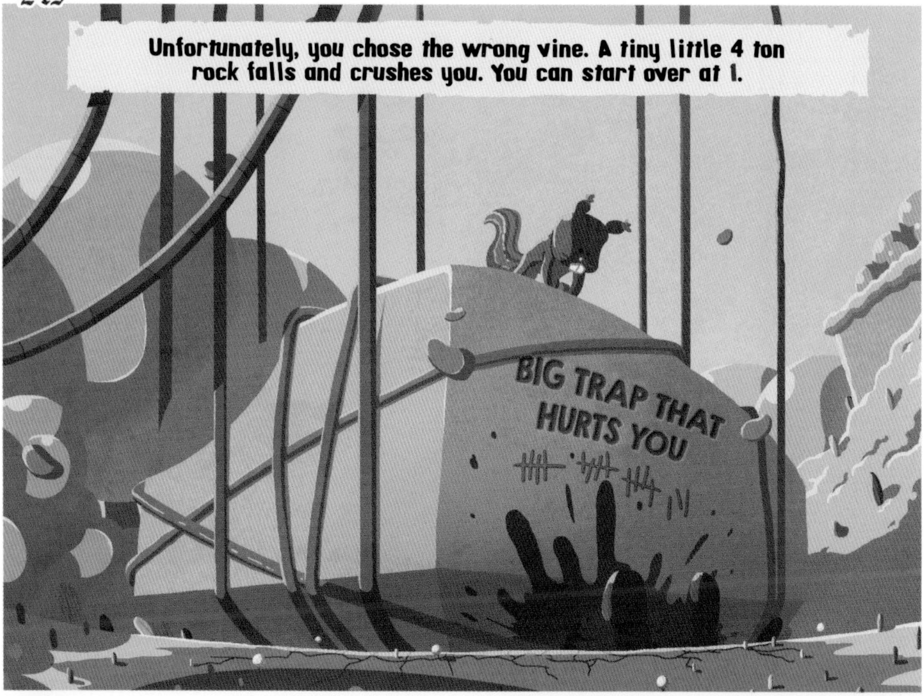
Unfortunately, you chose the wrong vine. A tiny little 4 ton rock falls and crushes you. You can start over at 1.
BIG TRAP THAT HURTS YOU

246

GOOD GRIEF! IT'S IMPOSSIBLE TO KNOW WHICH BRICKS TO USE. COULD YOU HELP ME? IF YOU FIGURE IT OUT, GO TO 38. OTHERWISE, LEAVE TO 292 SO I CAN CONCENTRATE.

247

NO BUT HEHE, IT'S OKAY? NOW GET OUTTA HERE. THOSE 10 GOLD PIECES DON'T GIVE YOU THE RIGHT TO RUMMAGE AROUND MY BOAT, AND CERTAINLY NOT MY ROOM! GET OUT, I DON'T WANT TO SEE YOU ANYMORE!
The captain chases you off his boat, very angry that you invaded his personal space. You're no longer welcome to return here. Go to 115.

248

WHO DARES DISTURB ME IN MY GLOOMY HOME? LEAVE HERE BEFORE I HURT YOU!
If you wish to fight, go to 335. To turn around and leave, go to 350. If you have the Hero's Amulet, go to 224.

249

137

250

HEHE! NOT BAD, FOR A HUMAN! HERE, TAKE THESE FEATHERS, THEY WILL PROVE THEMSELVES INDISPENSABLE.
Now return to 175.

251

197

252

107

253

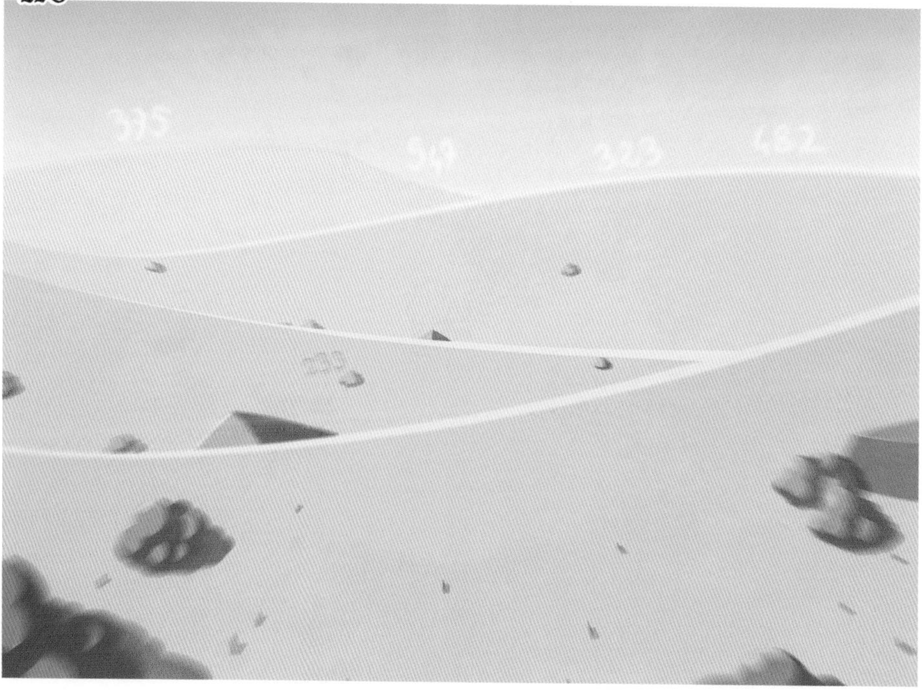

254

175

255

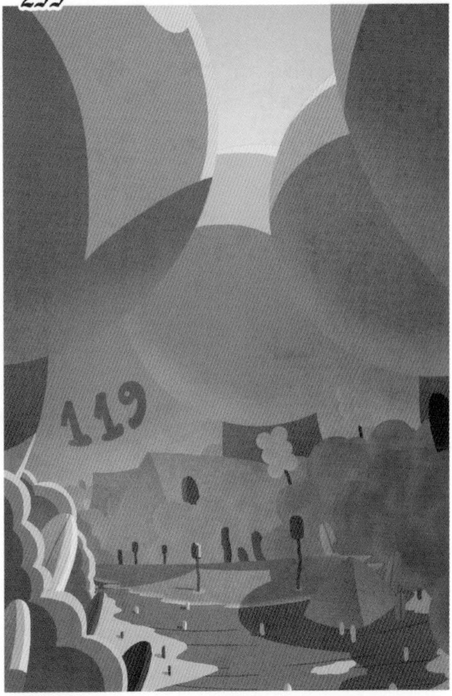
119

256

IF YOU HAVE ANY, I'LL BUY THE FLOWER BULBS FOR 10 GOLD PIECES EACH.
Once you've finished doing business, leave the cabin and go to 32.

257

If you can't get in, return to 350. If you have a magnifying glass, you can find the entrance between 18 and 19.
Here lies Lord Zorané
His Generosity was Great and Immeasurable

258

328

259

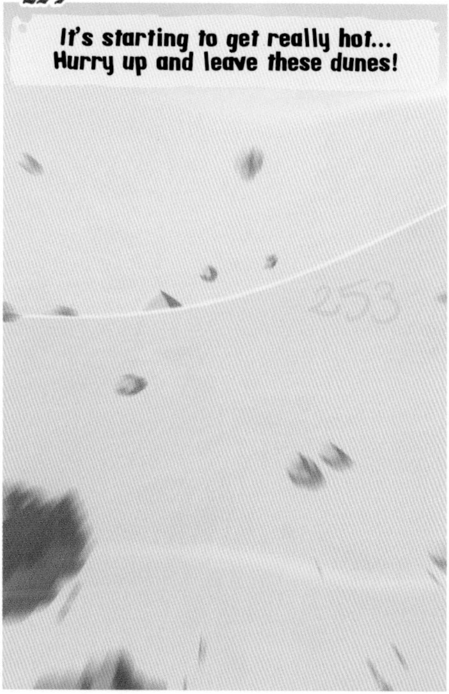
It's starting to get really hot...
Hurry up and leave these dunes!
253

260

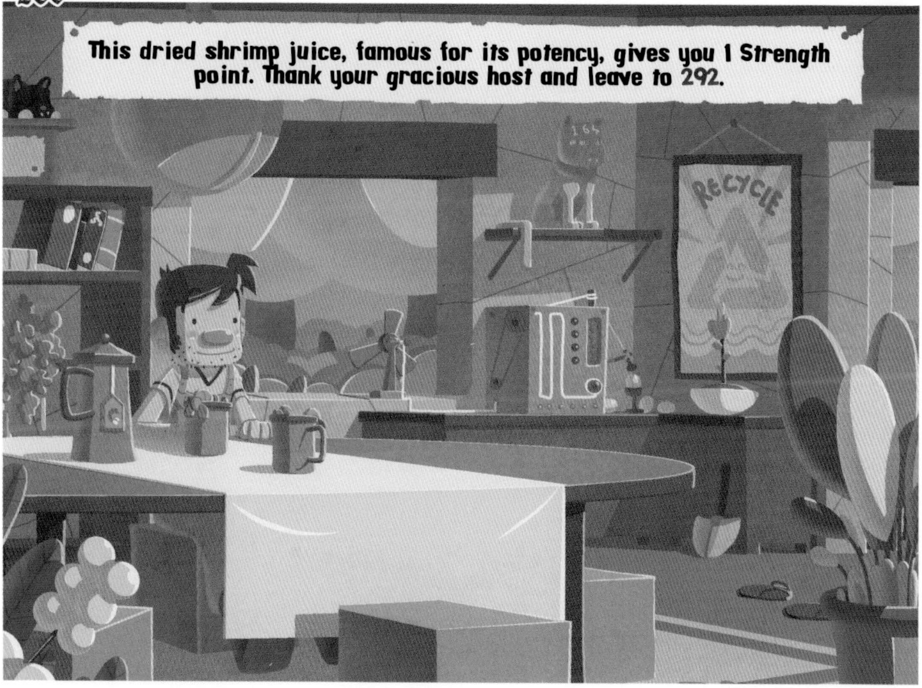
This dried shrimp juice, famous for its potency, gives you 1 Strength point. Thank your gracious host and leave to 292.
RECYCLE

261

HELLO, MY GOOD MAN! IF YOU HAVE THE REQUIRED COMPETENCE TO WIELD MY MAGNIFICENT WEAPONS, YOU CAN BUY ONE OF THEM FOR A MERE 5 GOLD PIECES. THEY HAVE ALL BEEN PRODUCED USING A VERY RARE ELEMENT THAT CAUSES THEM TO BE INCREDIBLY LIGHTWEIGHT, MEANING THEY WON'T WEIGH YOU DOWN AT ALL.
BOW & QUIVER & 10 ARROWS
AGILITY 13
INTELLIGENCE 13
STRENGTH 13
If you have the 5 gold pieces to spend, buy the weapon of your choice and return to 74.

262

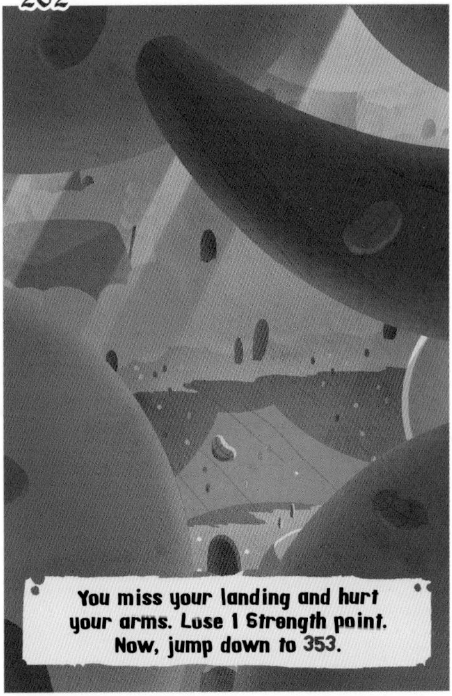
You miss your landing and hurt your arms. Lose 1 Strength point. Now, jump down to 353.

263

If you didn't cut branch E, leave immediately to 15. For that matter, leave even if you did cut the right branch: this kid isn't giving you anything.

264

321
178

265

235

266

1384

267

338

268

307

269

That little fool... err... man told you he was looking for three insects missing from his collection. You can help him, or leave to 240.
If you find the three insects, go to 129.

270

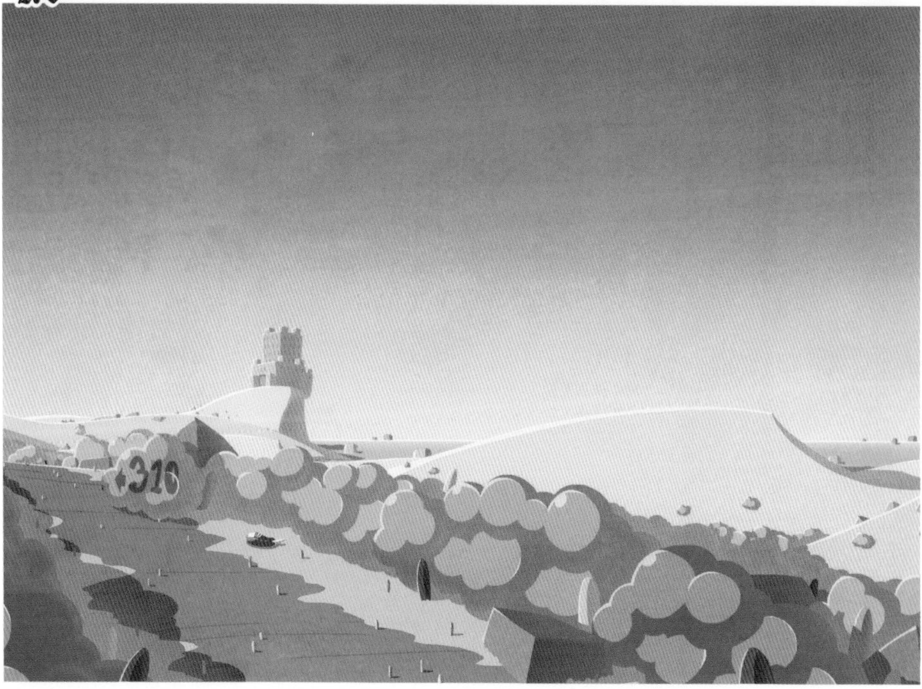
310

271

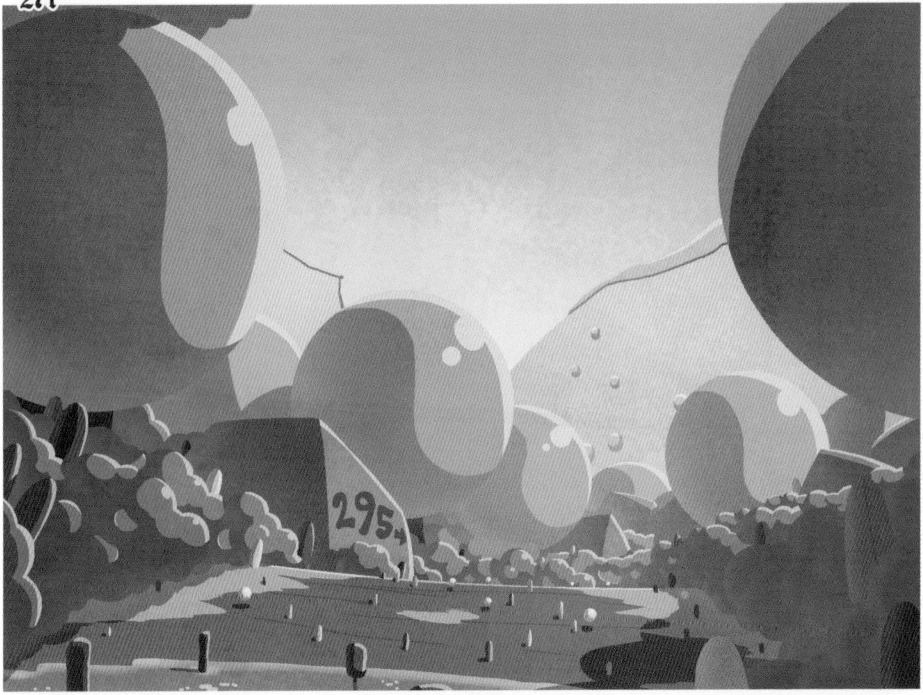
295

272

Note to self: a lone Thanaton... is never alone. You're about to die...
no use sticking around to watch. Restart at 1.

273

Ack! A malicious snake capable of hypnotizing you with a mere glance... you can leave to 194 if you have at least 10 Intelligence. Otherwise, you're dead and can restart at 1.

274

GREETINGS, NOBLE ADVENTURER. I SEE THAT MY TREASURES HAVE CAUGHT YOUR EYE: 200 GOLD PIECES AND YOU CAN TAKE WHICHEVER ONE YOU LIKE! OTHERWISE, COME TO 96 TO SEE WHAT ELSE I CAN OFFER YOU.

275

82
222

276

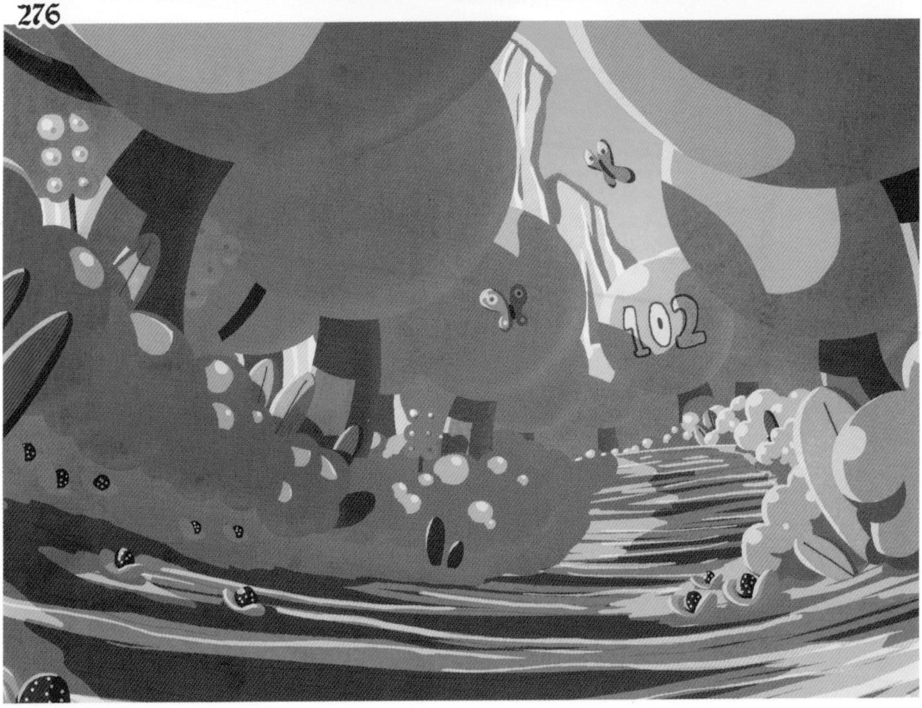
102

277

I probably don't have to tell you that this is going to hurt.
You should just go ahead and restart at 1.

278

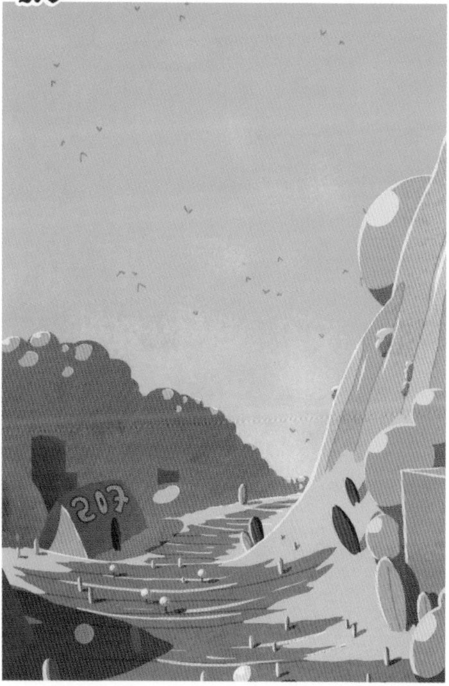
207

279

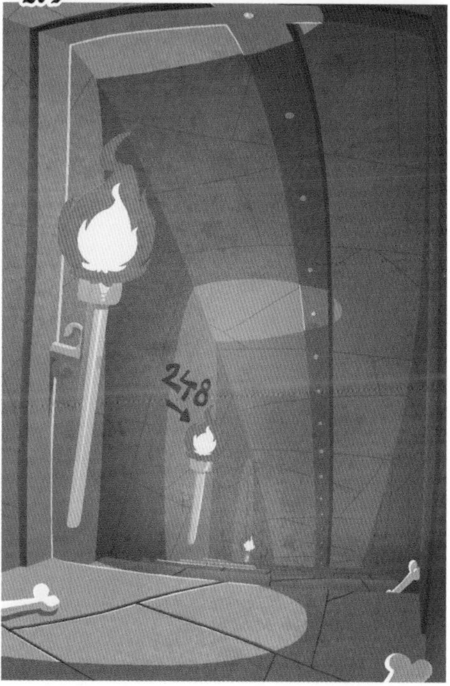
248

280

281

WHAT? REALLY? YOU'VE ALREADY FOUND THEM? THAT'S FANTASTIC! ALLOW ME TO THANK YOU... PLEASE, TAKE IT. I INSIST.
You made off well in this exchange, that's for sure! You've just received an old chicken in exchange for the beautiful ruby-laden ring that you found earlier. What luck! Now, go to 28.

282

IF YOU COME ACROSS THESE SYMBOLS, FOLLOW THEM.
= 6
= 1
Return to 153.

283

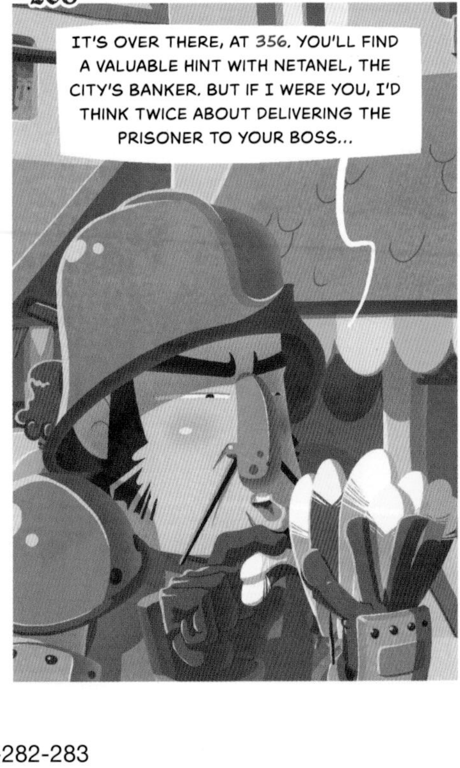

IT'S OVER THERE, AT 356. YOU'LL FIND A VALUABLE HINT WITH NETANEL, THE CITY'S BANKER. BUT IF I WERE YOU, I'D THINK TWICE ABOUT DELIVERING THE PRISONER TO YOUR BOSS...

284

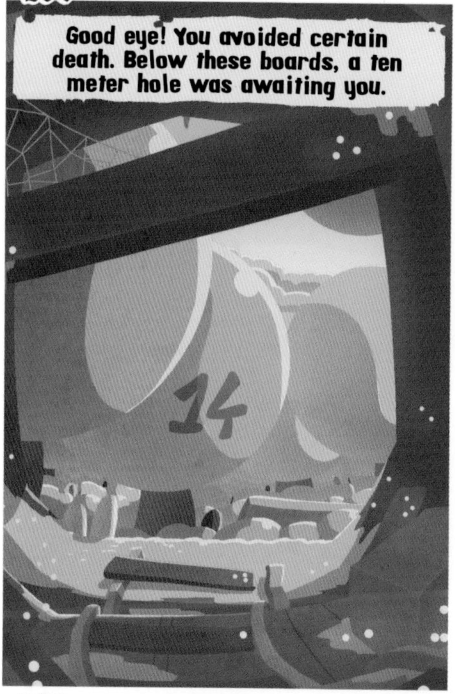
Good eye! You avoided certain death. Below these boards, a ten meter hole was awaiting you.
14

285

I WOULDN'T BE CAUGHT DEAD WRITING THIS KIND OF JUNK. IF YOU'RE LOOKING FOR AN AUTOGRAPH, SCRAM!

286

Unfortunately, you chose the wrong vine. A tiny little 4 ton rock falls and crushes you. You can start over at 1.
BIG TRAP THAT HURTS YOU

287

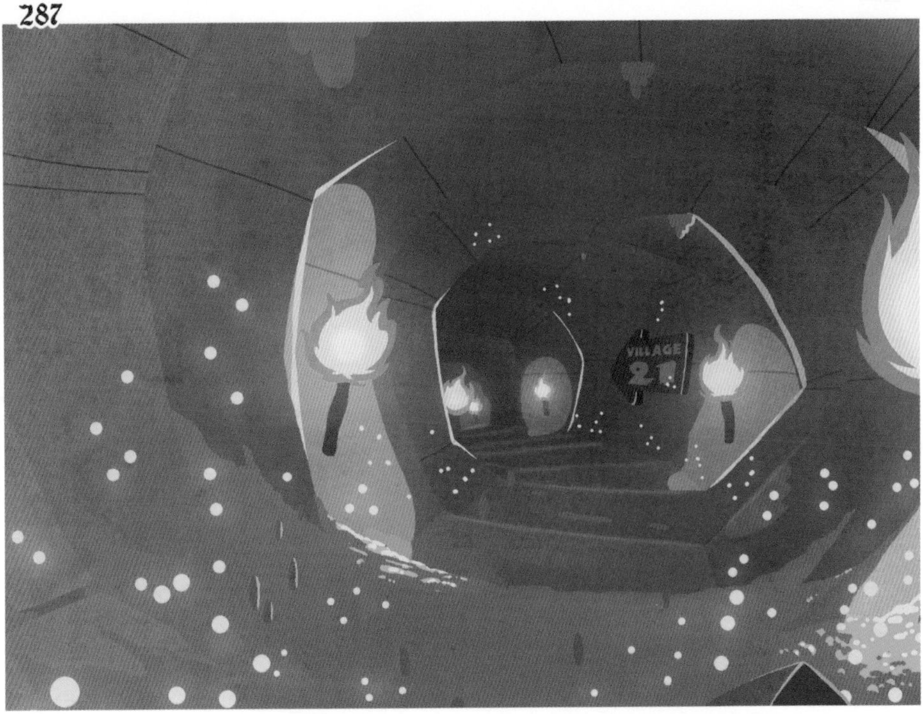
VILLAGE
21

288

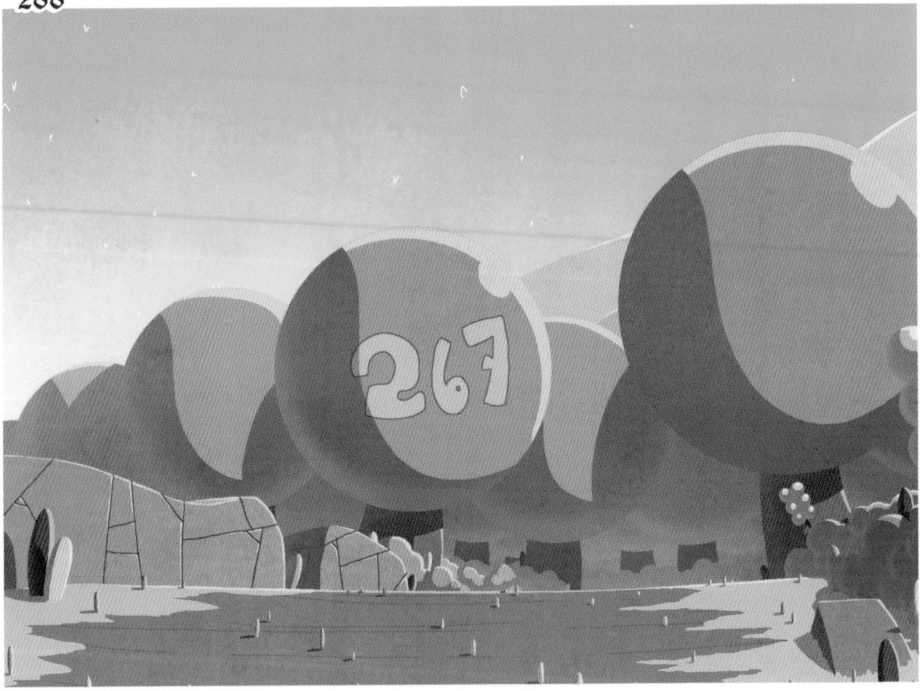
267

289

Not the warmest welcome! You can return to 74 if that's what your heart is telling you. Otherwise, step up and talk to the barkeep.
WE DON'T DO CREDIT... CASH ONLY!
158

290

How many times do I have to tell you to look before you leap. Those planks were rotten, and now you're dead! Restart your adventure at 1.

291

90
68

292

85

293

This beach is far from being the kind you see on postcards. You can continue along your path at 156.

294

295

304
153

296

189

297

Take this banana, it won't weigh anything in your bag.
If you see any others, take them. They're bound to come in handy.

298

R.I.P.
Clark Gabb
~97-12~
Forever In
Our Hearts
228

299

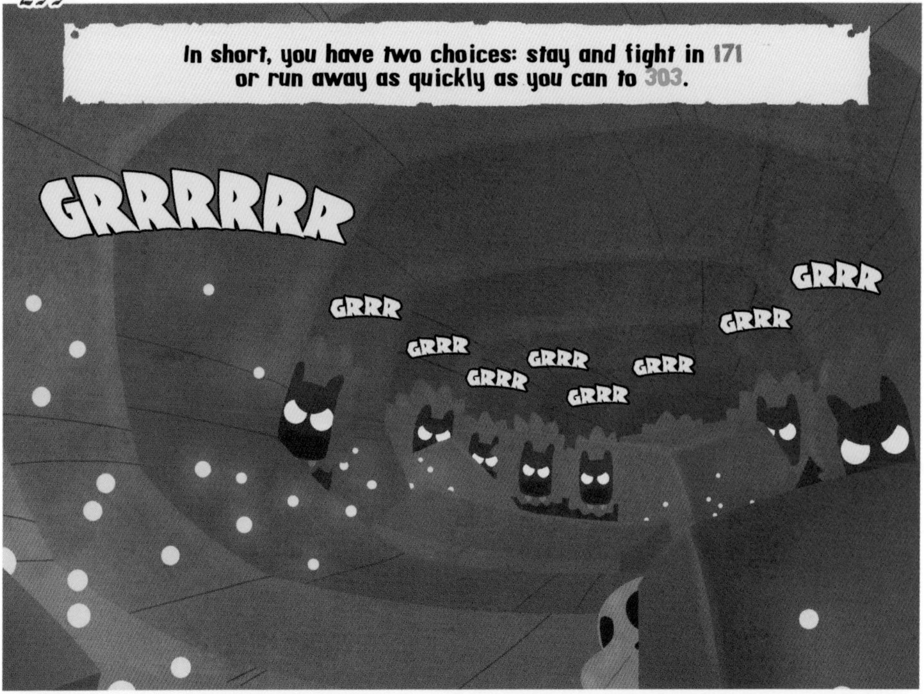
In short, you have two choices: stay and fight in 171 or run away as quickly as you can to 303.
GRRRRRR
GRRR
GRRR
GRRR
GRRR
GRRR
GRRR
GRRR
GRRR

300

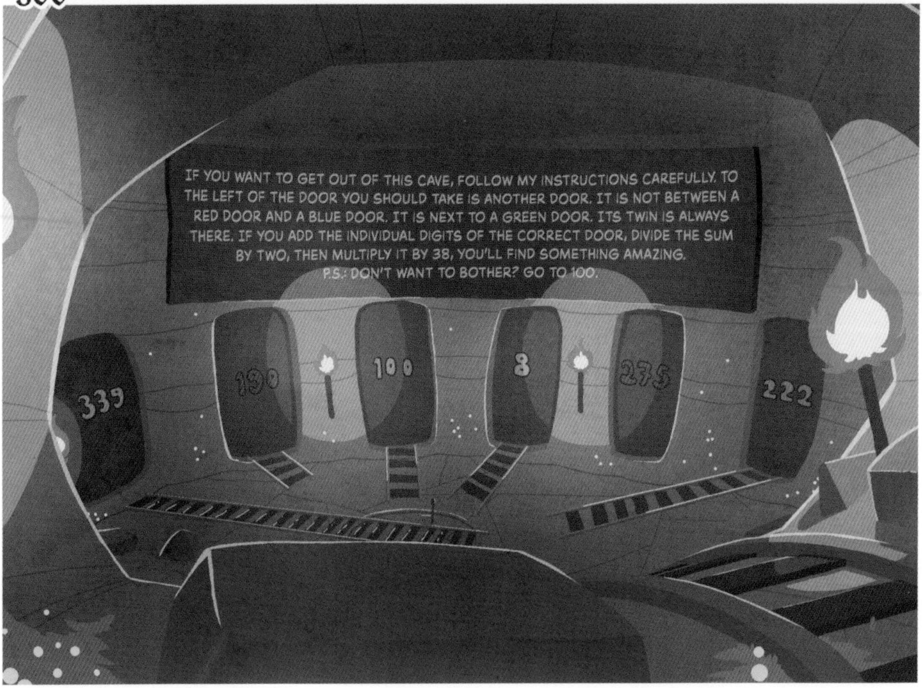
IF YOU WANT TO GET OUT OF THIS CAVE, FOLLOW MY INSTRUCTIONS CAREFULLY. TO THE LEFT OF THE DOOR YOU SHOULD TAKE IS ANOTHER DOOR. IT IS NOT BETWEEN A RED DOOR AND A BLUE DOOR. IT IS NEXT TO A GREEN DOOR. ITS TWIN IS ALWAYS THERE. IF YOU ADD THE INDIVIDUAL DIGITS OF THE CORRECT DOOR, DIVIDE THE SUM BY TWO, THEN MULTIPLY IT BY 38, YOU'LL FIND SOMETHING AMAZING.
P.S.: DON'T WANT TO BOTHER? GO TO 100.
339
190
100
8
275
222

301

39

302

220

303

209

304

VILLAGE
63
FOREST
81
295

305

If you have more than 14 Strength, you can lift the rock (if not, go to 226). It appears that you're being confronted by a terrible and menacing creature. If you are unarmed, it pinches you and you lose 2 points of Agility. However, if you have a weapon, you squash the crab instead, eat one of its pincers and gain 1 point of Strength. Now, head to 226.

306

214
251

307

274

308

You have no idea what this weird looking stone is supposed to do, but hold on to it. It doesn't weigh much, so it won't count against your Strength. Now, go to 254.

309

Your superior intellect allows you to see the puzzle more clearly. However, if you're still having trouble, just go to 175.

310

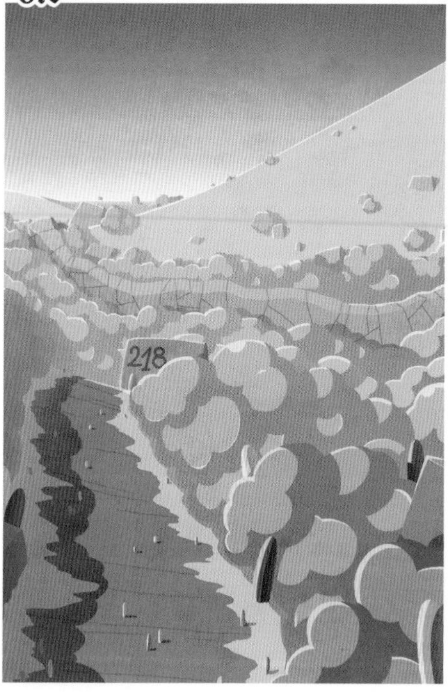
218

311

Well played: you've weakened him! Finish him at 157 or help him sit down at 229.
OWIE, OWIE, OWIE, OWIE... THAT REALLY HURT, JEEPERS!

80

313

BLAM
Ouch! Pay attention, for goodness' sake! You're in a swamp, not your grandma's backyard! The shock makes you lose a few neurons and 1 point of Intelligence. Continue to 131.

314

THE NAME'S AUSTER. AH! THAT THERE IS MY BIG BROTHER, AQUILIN. NOT EXACTLY A BARREL OF LAUGHS, BUT HONEST AND RELIABLE. OVER THERE IS MISTRAL, A LITTLE COLD, BUT GOOD AND KIND. AND FINALLY, HÉGOA. HE'S PRETTY UPSET RIGHT NOW. HE LOST THE RING OUR LATE FATHER LEFT TO HIM. YOU DIDN'T FIND IT, BY ANY CHANCE? IF YOU DID, HURRY TO 203, AND YOU'LL BE REWARDED. OTHERWISE, YOU CAN HEAD BACK TO 28.

315

COME CLOSER, STRANGER. INTERESTED IN A LITTLE GAME?
Water = 14
Banana Juice = 16
Dark Roast Coffee = 20
It's up to you. Play a game with the monkey in 205 or turn around to 175?

316

If your answer was "Pablo", you're safe and can head to 167. Otherwise, it's all over for you! You can restart your adventure at 1.

317

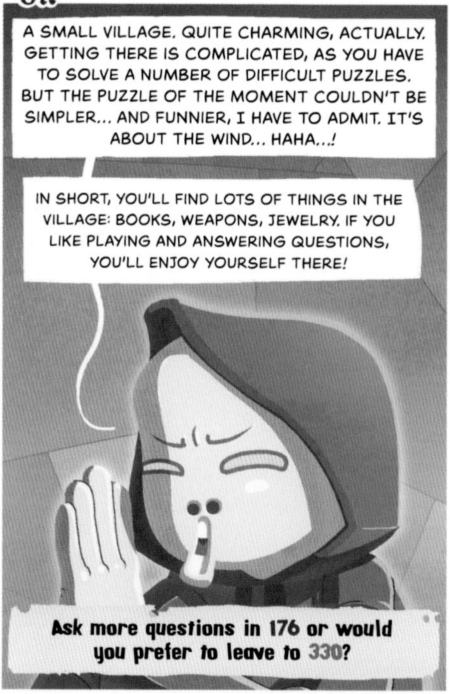
A SMALL VILLAGE. QUITE CHARMING, ACTUALLY. GETTING THERE IS COMPLICATED, AS YOU HAVE TO SOLVE A NUMBER OF DIFFICULT PUZZLES. BUT THE PUZZLE OF THE MOMENT COULDN'T BE SIMPLER... AND FUNNIER, I HAVE TO ADMIT. IT'S ABOUT THE WIND... HAHA...!
IN SHORT, YOU'LL FIND LOTS OF THINGS IN THE VILLAGE: BOOKS, WEAPONS, JEWELRY. IF YOU LIKE PLAYING AND ANSWERING QUESTIONS, YOU'LL ENJOY YOURSELF THERE!
Ask more questions in 176 or would you prefer to leave to 330?

318

319

181

320

Wow! A magnificent necklace that adds 1 point to each of your characteristics, as well as 2 points of intuition. Intuition? What's that supposed to mean? While you're thinking about it, return to 218.
Pirates

321

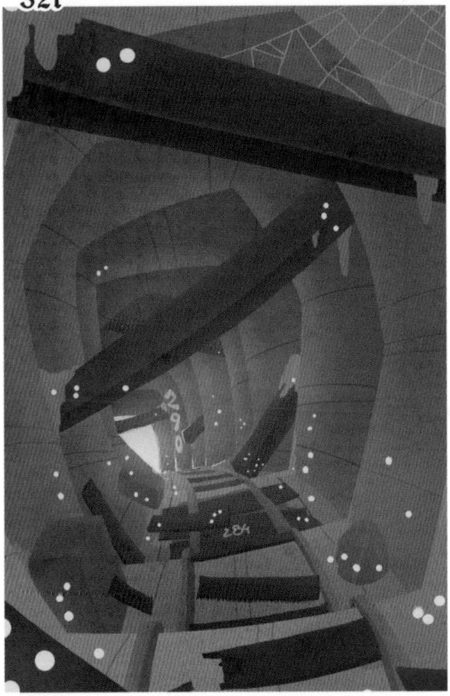
290
284

322

If you'd like to go to sea, turn to 37
Otherwise, return to 115

323

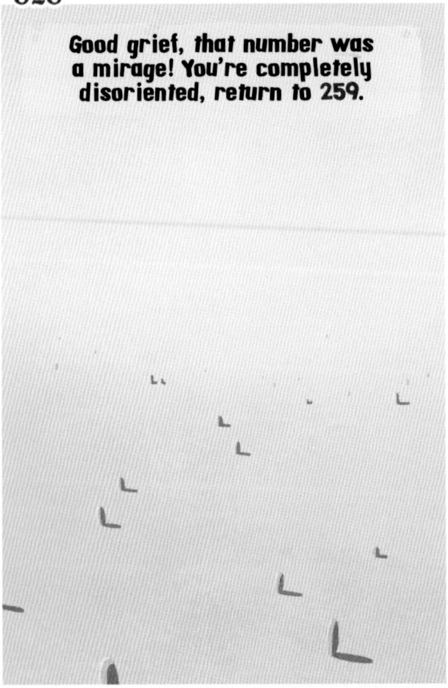
Good grief, *that* number was a mirage! You're completely disoriented, return to 259.

324

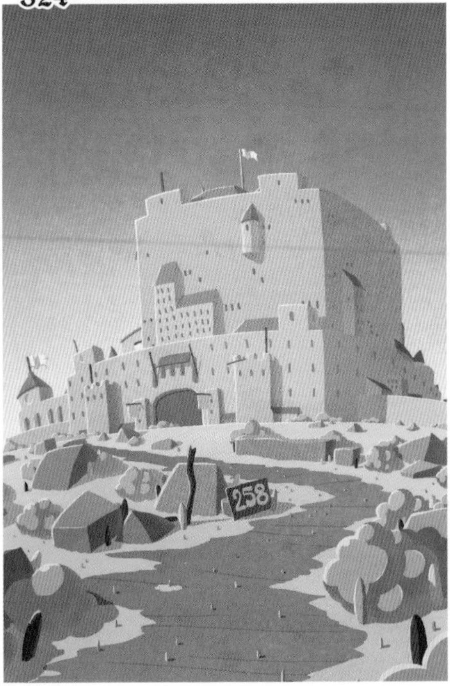
258

325

115

326

71
100

327

If you have fewer than 11 points of Agility, your big sausage-like fingers won't be able to catch that card. Return to 153.
282

328

355

329

243

330

AH YES, I UNDERSTAND. IT ISN'T EASY TO LIVE IN COLD, DARK CAVES LIKE THIS. FOLLOW ME, I'LL SHOW YOU THE WAY OUT IN 143!

331

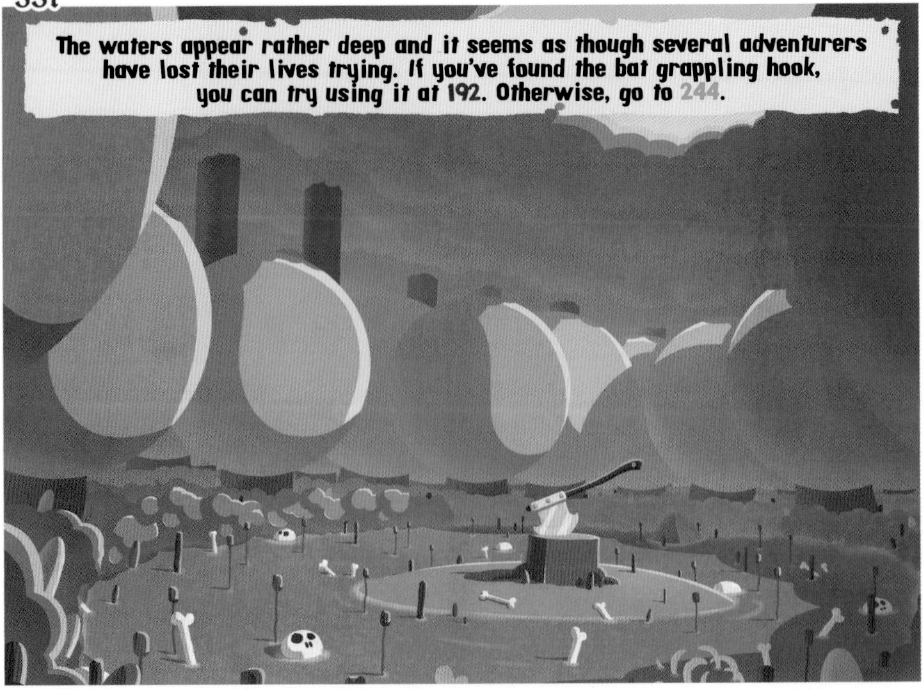
The waters appear rather deep and it seems as though several adventurers have lost their lives trying. If you've found the bat grappling hook, you can try using it at 192. Otherwise, go to 244.

332

HMMM... YES, THAT RINGS A BELL. I BELIEVE THAT GILLAM, IN THE VILLAGE OF BANDITS, COULD TELL YOU MORE. IT'S AT THE WEST END OF THE ISLAND. IF YOU SEE HIM, TELL HIM THAT PABLO SENT YOU. THAT'LL PUT A SMILE ON HIS FACE.
If you'd like to know more about the village of bandits, go to 317. If you want to learn more about the Thanatons, go to 176. If you'd like to be shown the way out of this stuffy cave, go to 330.

333

AH, GOOD... SEE FOR YOURSELF.
ONE OBJECT = ONE STRAWBERRY
ONE OBJECT = 3 STRAWBERRIES + 1 WHITE FLOWER
+1 AGIL
If you have the required objects, you can exchange them for a corresponding object. You may perform as many exchanges as you like. When you're done, return to 176.

334

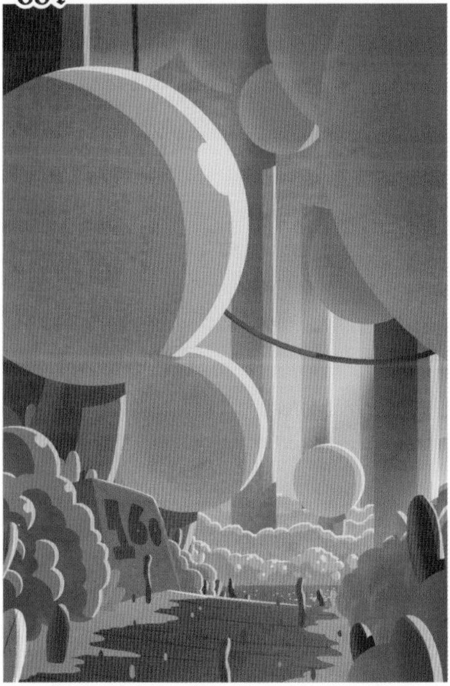

335

To defeat the lord, hit him in the radius. If you fail, you'll have to restart your adventure at 1, due to the whole death by scimitar thing. Good luck!
EN GARDE, BRIGAND!

336

328

337

TAKE EVERYTHING: BAG, WEAPONS, JEWELRY.
CONSIDER YOURSELF LUCKY THAT I'M NOT TOSSING YOU IN THE DUNGEON, VERMIN!
And just like *that*, you're as naked as a jaybird. You've lost all of *the* objects you found on your adventure... Now, go to 356.

338

348

339

Unable to see anything, you decide to light a torch. In hindsight, this wasn't the best idea, as it turns out you're in a room full of explosives. We'll spare you the gruesome details, but rest assured, there was an earth-shattering KABOOM! You can restart your adventure at 1.
DANGER!
PLAN
TNT
TNT
DANGER

340

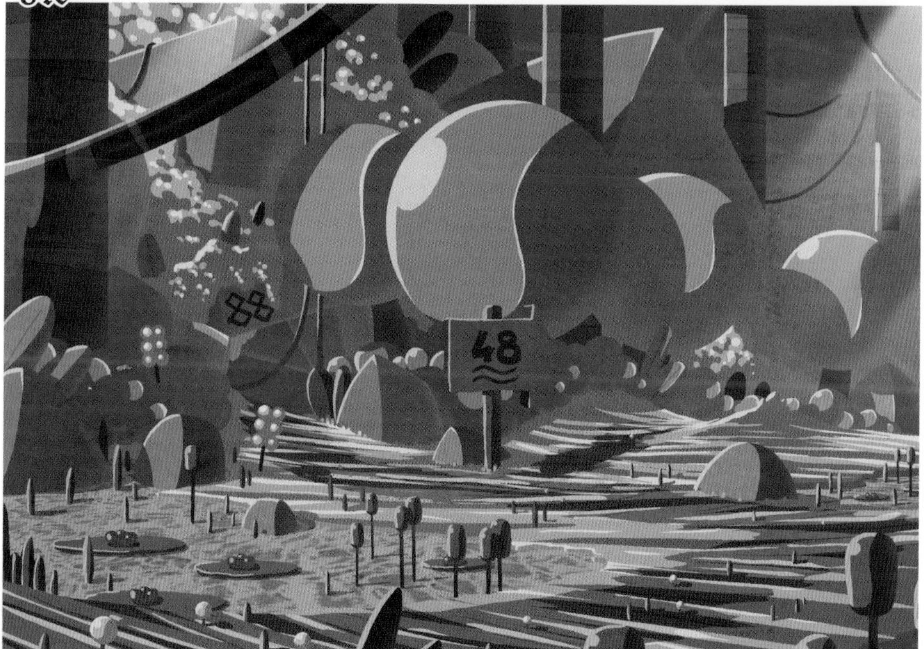
48

341

294
161

342

HELP YOU OUT OF HERE? OBVIOUSLY I CAN! TAKE THIS FEATHER AND EITHER HEAD WEST TO 211 OR EAST AT 262. IT'S LIGHT AS A FEATHER, SO IT WON'T COUNT TOWARDS YOUR WEIGHT LIMIT.

343

237

344

37

345

34

346

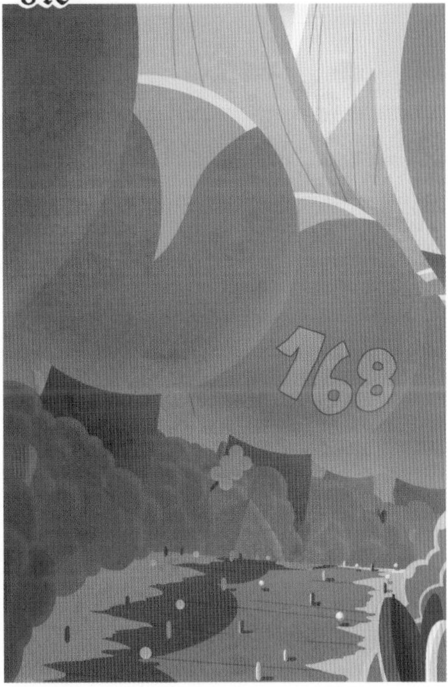
168

347

ALTITUDE
1750 M
172

348

182

349

SO, YOU'VE WASHED UP ON THIS ISLAND AND YOU'RE LOOKING FOR YOUR FRIEND!
SEE, IT'S FUNNY, BECAUSE THE LAST GUY WHO CAME THROUGH HERE TOLD US THE SAME THING. TELL YOU WHAT... ANSWER THIS PUZZLE, AND WE'LL SHOW YOU WHICH WAY HE WENT.

I'M GREEN, I COME FROM A TREE, AND I CAN ALSO BE RED, YELLOW OR BROWN... WHAT AM I?
I'LL GIVE YOU THE ANSWER IN 17 SECONDS.

350

←238
257→
RIP

351

SIR, MY FISHING LINE IS ALL TANGLED...
I'M SCARED TO CUT THE WRONG
BRANCH. CAN YOU HELP ME?
If you know which branch to cut, that won't just make the problem worse, go to 263. If you'd rather not take on such an onerous responsibility, go to 15, or to 29 to go back from where you came.

352

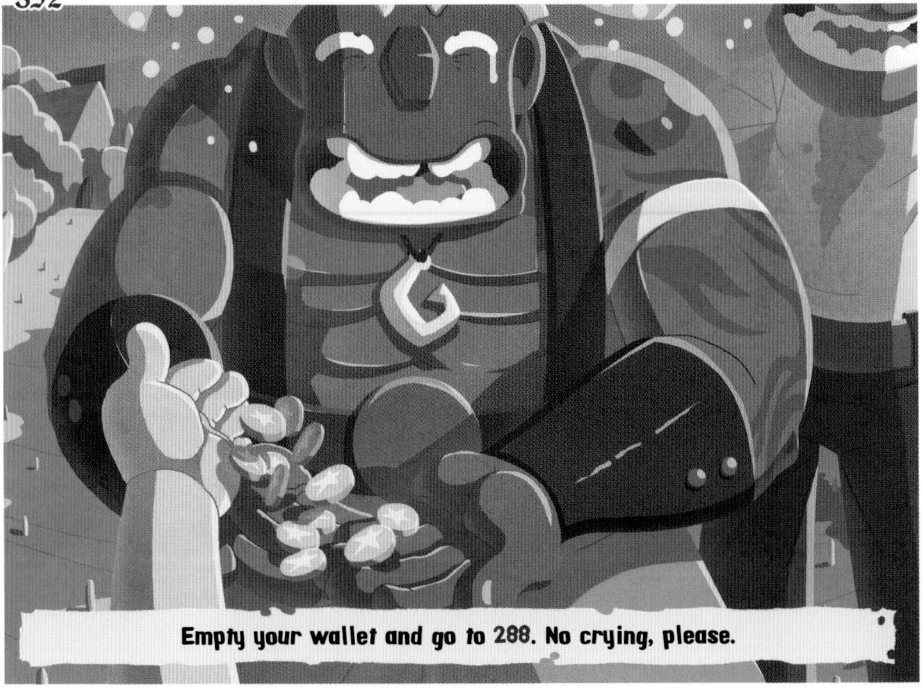
Empty your wallet and go to 288. No crying, please.

353

140
28

354

YEP... I SHOULD HAVE KNOWN. ONCE A PICKLE, ALWAYS A PICKLE. YOU SHOULD GET GOING NOW. JEAN-MICHEL IS A LITTLE TENSE AT THE MOMENT. IT WOULD BE A SHAME IF YOU ENDED UP WITH AN ARROW STICKING OUT OF YOUR RIGHT EYE.
353

HALT,
PIRATE VERMIN!
ARE YOU THE SCUM THAT'S OUT TO FIND THE MAN WITH THE GOLDEN FINGERS?
DON'T YOU LIE TO ME: YOU KNOW VERY WELL WHAT I'M TALKING ABOUT!

SO, YOU'RE TELLING ME YOU DON'T KNOW HIS SECRET?
HA HA! YOU IDIOT! ONLY A PIRATE WOULD RISK THEIR LIFE SEARCHING FOR A MAN THEY KNOW NOTHING ABOUT!
LISTEN WELL, I HAVE A PROPOSITION FOR YOU.
I'M A FEATHER COLLECTOR. GIVE ME 10 FEATHERS AND I'LL LET YOU LEAVE AND KEEP LOOKING... EVEN BETTER: I'LL GIVE YOU A CLUE TO HELP YOU FIND HIM...
OTHERWISE, I'LL CONFISCATE ALL OF YOUR BELONGINGS AND LEAVE YOU SCRAMBLING TO FIND YOUR MAN... SO?
IF YOU HAVE 10 FEATHERS TO GIVE TO THE MAN -- AND THAT YOU WOULD LIKE TO OFFER -- GO TO 283. OTHERWISE, HEAD TO 337.

Congratulations! After searching the island from top to bottom, you can now be certain that your fugitive is somewhere in this city. If you want to get your hands on him and find out what he's hiding, it's time to crack open Pirates: The City of Skulls!